HOW DOES A CUT HEAL?

WHAT ARE FRECKLES

WHAT ARE YOU MADE OF?

WHAT MAKES BLOOD RED?

bloodcells

Do boys have more muscles than girls?

DO YOU NEED YOUR TONSILS? No

CAN YOU SWALLOW STANDING ON YOUR HEAD? no

YOU GET A CAVITY? eating sweets

What happens when you breathe?
your lungs move

What are black-and-blue marks?

EYE LIKE A CAMERA?
they both focus

HOW DO YOU HEAR?

HOW LONG DOES IT TAKE TO DIGEST A MEAL?

through his stethoscope?

THE QUESTION AND ANSWER BOOK

RANDOM HOUSE

THE HUMAN BODY

WHY DO YOU SLEEP?

How is your heart like a powerful pump?
yes

The Question and Answer Book About The Human Body

by Ann McGovern

Illustrated by Lorelle M. Raboni

Random House, New York

Without your questions, I wouldn't have written the answers.
So thank you

Lisa, Josh and Eli Langner
Susie and Chris Atran
Mia and Marco Runanin
Cathy Mesaric

The author, the artist and the publisher wish to thank Dr. Fleur Strand, Assistant Professor of Biology at New York University, for her valuable suggestions in connection with the preparation of the text and illustrations for this book.

This title was originally cataloged by the Library of Congress as follows: McGovern, Ann. The question and answer book about the human body. Illustrated by Lorelle M. Raboni. New York, Random House [1965] 68 p. illus. (part col.) 29 cm. 1. Physiology—Juvenile literature. 2. Anatomy, Human—Juvenile literature. i. Raboni, Lorelle M., illus. ii. Title. iii. Title: The human body. QP37.M33 j 612 65—19133 ISBN: 0-394-80780-4 ISBN: 0-394-90780-9 (lib. bdg.)

Contents

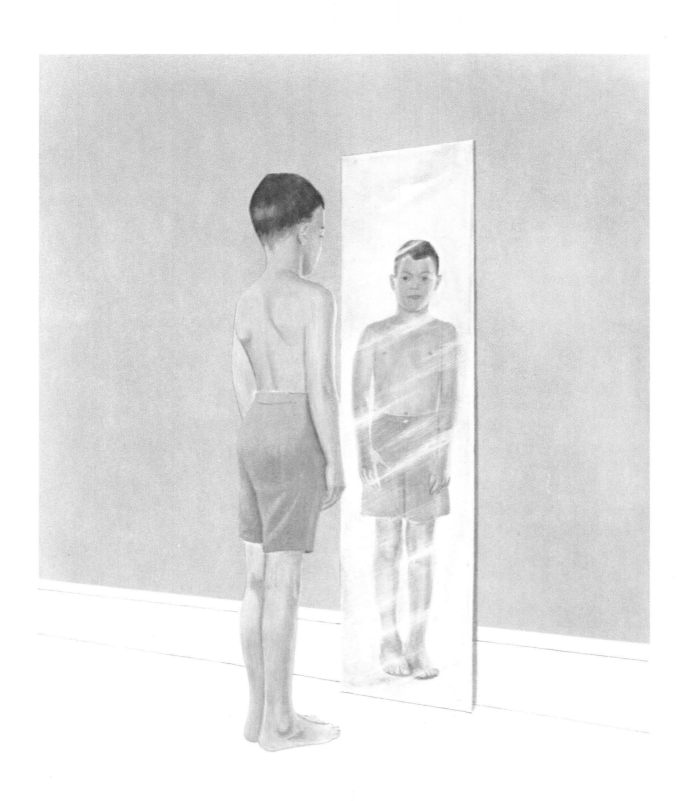

What Makes You <u>You</u>

WHAT ARE YOU MADE OF?

Look in the mirror. You see your ears, nose, arms, legs, hands, feet. Yet what you can see is only a small part of you. Beneath your skin, inside of you, there are bones and muscles, heart, brain, and lungs, and all the other parts that keep your body working.

Stroke your arm. That's soft. Touch your wrist. That's hard. Soft skin, hard bones—every part of you is made up of cells. Your body is made up of billions and billions of living cells.

Your cells are very, very tiny and can be seen only under a microscope.

Most cells are built in the same way. A thin, delicate *membrane* surrounds the cell. Inside the cell is a living material called *protoplasm*. Many different substances make up the protoplasm of a cell.

Inside every cell is its very important *nucleus*. It is the nucleus that makes it possible for cells to split in half. Each new cell is formed with its own nucleus, protoplasm, and surrounding membrane.

The cells in your body need food, since every cell is alive.

Have you ever heard the rhyme which says that little girls are made of "sugar and spice and everything nice" or that little boys are made of "snips and snails and puppy dog tails?" It's not so! Little girls, little boys, *everyone* is made of cells.

ARE ALL YOUR CELLS ALIKE?

The cells in your body are of many kinds, many sizes, many shapes. Your bones are made of one kind of cell, your muscles of another kind, your skin of still another. There are at least six different kinds of cells in your blood alone.

Different kinds of cells do different

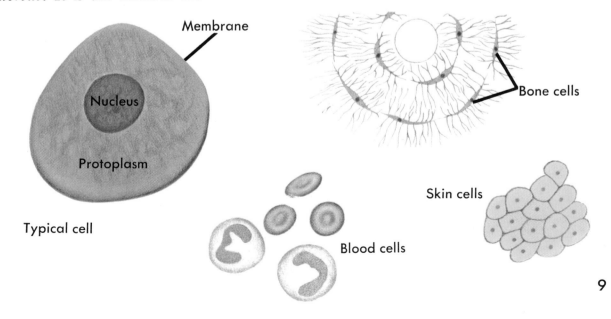

Membrane

Nucleus

Protoplasm

Typical cell

Bone cells

Blood cells

Skin cells

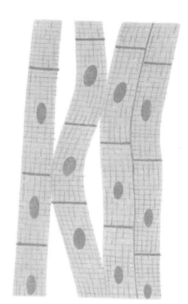

Three types of muscle cells

jobs. A group of one kind of cell makes up your muscle tissue. Muscle cells are formed so that they can tighten and relax to make your body move. No other cells can do what the muscle cells do. A group of another kind of cells makes up your nerve tissue. These can send messages to your brain from other parts of your body. No other cells can do that special job.

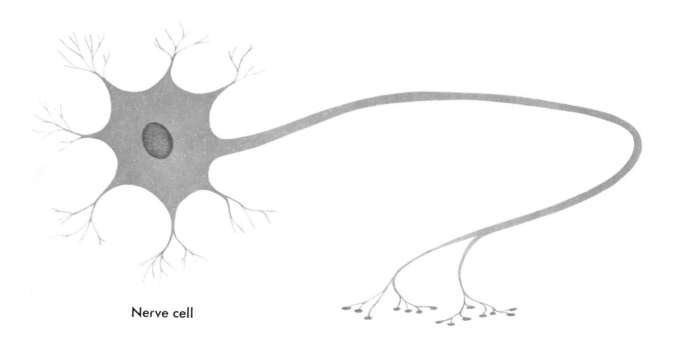

Nerve cell

How You Grow

HOW DO YOU GROW?

You grow because the cells of your body keep making new cells. A cell grows. When it is fully grown, it divides in two. Then each of these two cells divide, making four cells, and so on.

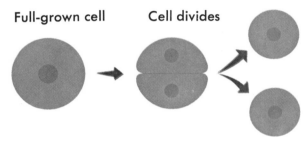

Full-grown cell   Cell divides

    The cells that make up your bones, for instance, divide to make new bone cells. That's how your bones grow. The same thing happens with the cells that make up other parts of your body.

    Some cells seem to act differently. Your brain cells grow larger after you are born, but they do not divide to make new cells.

    Your body uses up cells constantly. Everytime you scrape your skin, for example, you scrape off thousands of skin cells. New skin cells are being made all the time to take the place of those that were scraped away.

    Every second, night and day, your cells are growing and dividing, and growing and dividing, again and again. That is how you grow. Asleep or awake, your cells grow and divide, over and over and over.

WHEN DID YOU START TO GROW?

You are made of billions and billions of living cells. But before you were born, you started to grow from just one cell. This special cell was formed when a cell from your father, called a *sperm* cell, joined with a cell from your mother called an *egg* cell. This special cell is called a *fertilized* egg. From this one special cell came all the cells that make up a human body.

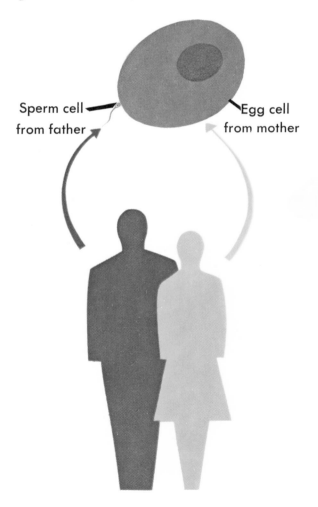

Sperm cell from father

Egg cell from mother

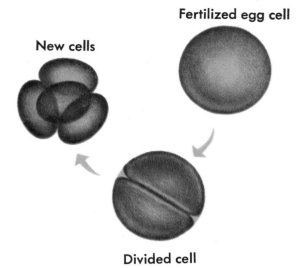

Fertilized egg cell

New cells

Divided cell

A human being begins with one fertilized egg cell. This cell divides to form all the cells needed to make up the different parts of the body. Before a baby is born, many changes take place in the growing embryo. Some of these changes are shown below.

The special cell divided and became two cells. And the two new cells divided again. And again. From that first cell came all your cells—your muscle cells, your skin cells, nerve cells, blood cells, and many others.

A baby, before it is born, is called an *embryo*. When you were an embryo you grew inside your mother's body for nine months until you were big enough to be born.

A two-month old embryo already has eyes, nose, ears, and mouth. It has tiny legs and arms, too, and a heart that beats and sends blood through its body.

When you were a six-month-old embryo, you had eyebrows and eyelashes. A month later, hair began to grow on your head. All this time, for nine months, you were gaining weight and growing. When you were born, you probably weighed from six to nine pounds and were about twenty inches long.

A complete human being grew from that one special cell!

After nine months all parts of the embryo have developed completely and the baby is ready to be born.

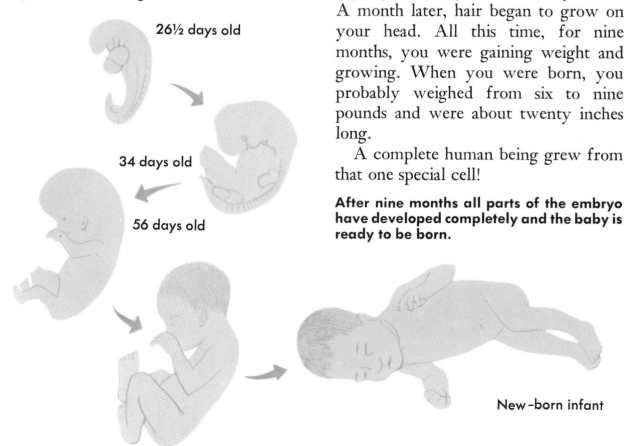

26½ days old

34 days old

56 days old

Between 5 and 6 months old

New-born infant

WHEN WILL YOU STOP GROWING?

Girls reach their full height when they are about 18 years old. Boys keep growing taller for a few more years. When you reach your full size you may get fatter, but you won't grow any taller.

There are two times in your life when you grow very fast. The first time was right after you were born and it lasted until you were about six months old. You will start to grow very fast again when you reach your early teens. Girls grow faster than boys until they get to be teenagers. Teenage boys catch up and then grow faster and stronger.

Your head stops growing earlier than the rest of you. When you were a newborn baby, you looked as if you were almost all head! By the time you are ten, your head is nearly full size.

The bones of your arms and legs were short when you were a baby. At the age of nine or ten, they start to grow longer rapidly, and they keep growing until you reach your full height.

Growing taller is only one way in which you grow. Your body changes in other ways. When a boy is about 13 years old, his voice begins to get deeper and he may have the beginnings of a beard. At the age of 13 or 14 a girl's body begins to look like that of a woman's. And inside the bodies of both girls and boys, important changes are taking place —changes that make it possible for a girl and a boy, when they are older, to become a mother and father.

In the early teens many changes take place in both boys and girls.

7 years   13 years

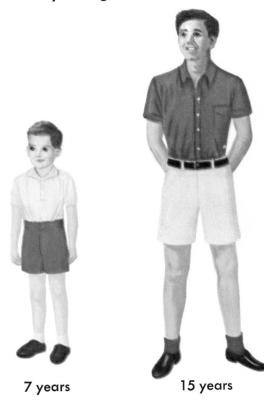

7 years   15 years

Your Marvelous Skeleton

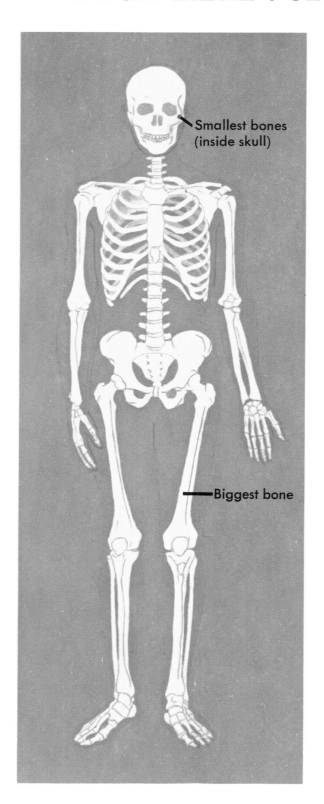

Smallest bones
(inside skull)

Biggest bone

WHAT HOLDS YOU UP?

Without a framework a house would fall apart. Without a framework you would fall apart, too.

In addition to your bones, your muscles, joints and ligaments form the framework of your body. Without these supports your body would collapse into a pile of odd bones, just as the framework of a house would collapse without its nails, hinges, and joints.

From the top of your head to the tip of your toes, you have 206 bones of different shapes and sizes. You have long bones in your arms and legs, short bones in your fingers and toes. You have flat bones in your head and hips and in your shoulder blades.

What are your biggest bones? Your strong thighbones. Your smallest? The three tiny bones in your ear, inside your head. These bones look like their names —the *hammer*, the *anvil*, and the *stirrup*.

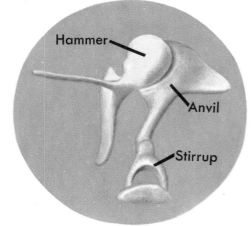

Hammer

Anvil

Stirrup

These three tiny bones in the ear fit into the small space indicated by the red dot in the head of the figure at the left.

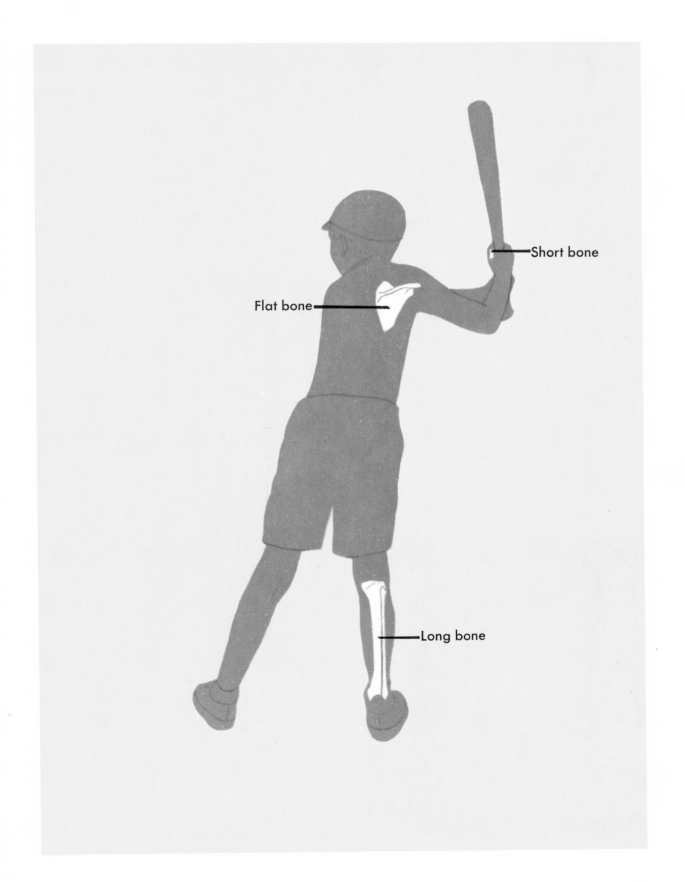

Short bone

Flat bone

Long bone

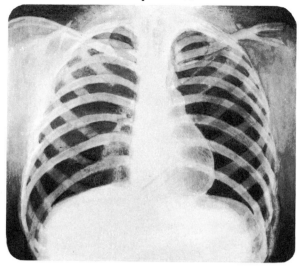

X-ray of ribs

HOW CAN YOU SEE YOUR BONES?

You can't—without an X-ray picture. Many doctors have X-ray machines that take pictures of the hard parts inside your body. If your doctor should ever take an X-ray picture of you, ask him to show you the shadowy outlines of your bones.

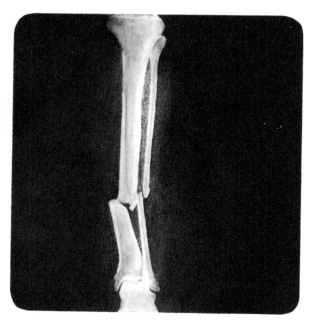

X-ray of broken leg bone

A doctor often has to take an X-ray picture to see where a bone is broken so that he will know how to set it.

WHAT DO YOUR BONES LOOK LIKE?

You have seen the bones dogs chew. Your bones are somewhat like that, but they are different shapes and sizes.

On the outside, your bones are white and hard and strong. On the inside, toward the ends they are spongy and filled with a soft tissue called *marrow*. Red blood cells are made in the red marrow. The center of a bone is hollow and filled with yellow marrow, which is mostly fat.

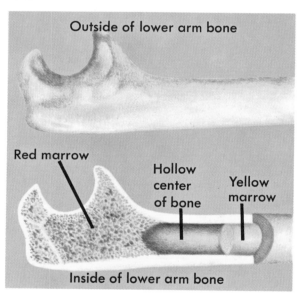

Outside of lower arm bone

Red marrow

Hollow center of bone

Yellow marrow

Inside of lower arm bone

WHAT'S SO FUNNY ABOUT A "FUNNY BONE"?

Ouch! You hit your "funny bone"—but you don't feel like laughing.

Your "funny bone" is a spot at the back of your elbow. When you bang it, you are really hitting a nerve that is close to the bone. You feel a strange tingling sensation that is different from the sensation you feel when you hit any other bone.

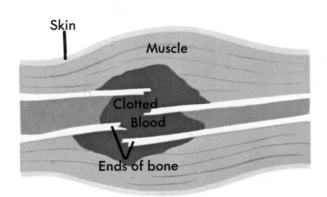

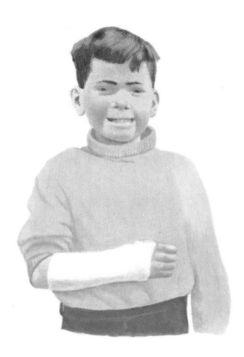

HOW DOES A BROKEN BONE HEAL?

A broken bone can heal all by itself. But in order for the bone to heal better, the doctor usually puts a splint or a cast around the break. This keeps the broken ends in the right place as the bone heals, and gives the new bone proper support.

Thickened blood, called *clotted* blood, from the broken blood vessels surrounds the two broken ends of the bone. This blood clot provides a network of *fibers* for the bone cells to begin to make new bone. The bone cells make a thick, bony swelling around the two broken ends. As soon as the swelling around the two broken ends is thick

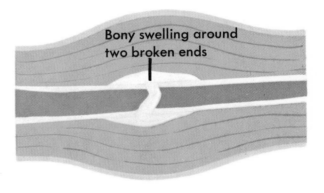

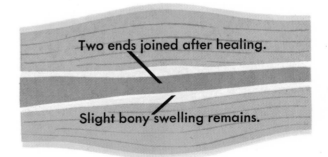

enough to heal the break completely, the body stops making new bone cells.

The bone is repaired so well that X-ray pictures may not even show where it was broken.

HOW ARE YOUR BONES JOINED TOGETHER?

Your bones are connected in different ways. The place where one bone is joined to another is called a *joint*. Your leg and knee are connected in the same way as your arm and elbow—with a *hinge joint*.

You can throw a ball overhand or swing your partner in a square dance because of the *ball-and-socket joints* in your shoulders and hips. Hinge joints and ball-and-socket joints allow you to move in many directions.

Your joints have to be as well oiled as the joints and hinges in a machine. But unlike a machine, your joints have their own supply of fluid which helps your bones move easily.

Some of your joints don't move. There are several joints in your skull, but your lower jaw is the only one that can move. If your lower jaw couldn't move, you couldn't chew your food, or talk, or laugh.

Your joints, muscles, and bones allow you to point your finger or bend down to tie your shoelace or do the hundreds of things you do every day when you move.

At the right are some of the different kinds of joints in your body.

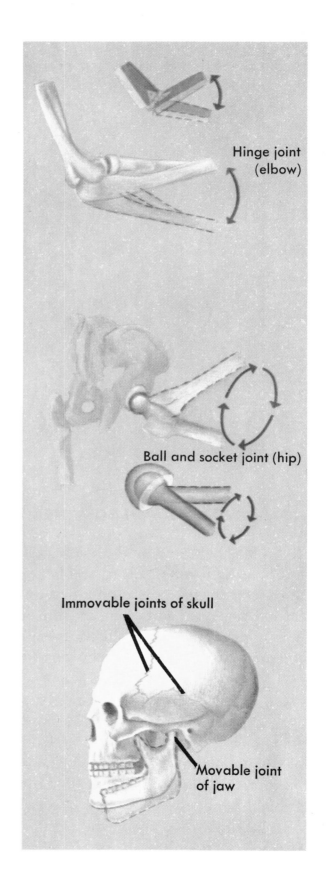

Hinge joint (elbow)

Ball and socket joint (hip)

Immovable joints of skull

Movable joint of jaw

Your Body's Movers—Your Muscles

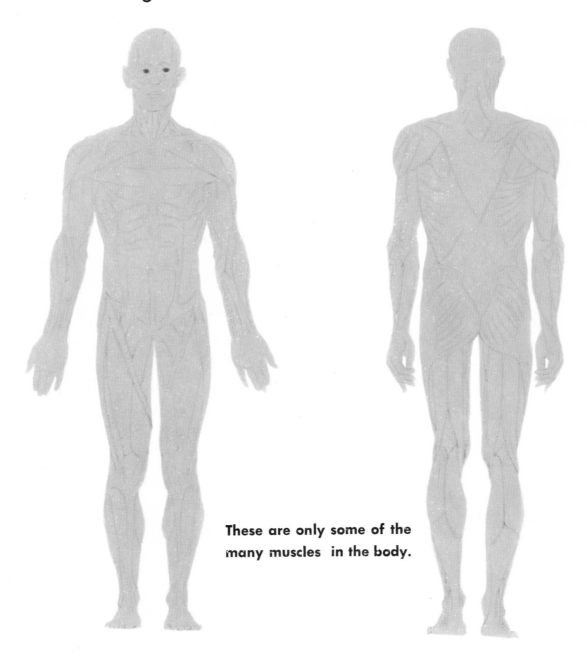

These are only some of the many muscles in the body.

HOW ARE YOU ABLE TO MOVE?

You need muscles in order to move. Every one of your 206 bones is covered by muscle.

Muscles are made of cells, like every part of your body. There are different kinds and shapes of muscle cells for different parts of you. But all muscle cells work the same way. They can all *contract*. When they contract, they tighten up and shorten. This pulls a bone and makes the bone move.

Like rubber bands, muscles can't push; they can only pull. Muscles work with other muscles to make you move. Bend your arm and straighten it. One group of muscles pulled your forearm up. Another group pulled it down.

Some muscles perform functions other than moving your bones. For instance, the muscles of your heart do a very important job without moving any bones —instead they force the blood through your body.

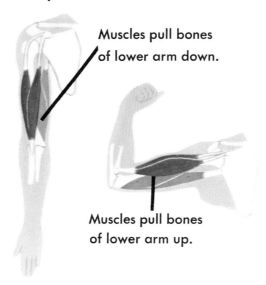

Muscles pull bones of lower arm down.

Muscles pull bones of lower arm up.

CAN YOU CONTROL ALL YOUR MUSCLES?

When you throw a ball you use muscles you can control. These are called *voluntary* muscles.

You also have *involuntary* muscles over which you have no control.

The muscles that help to digest your food are involuntary. They work without your even thinking about them. Your heart is another such muscle. Day and night, every minute, it beats to pump the blood through your body.

DO BOYS HAVE MORE MUSCLES THAN GIRLS?

Some boys may think they have more muscles than girls, but they haven't. Everyone has the same number of muscles—more than 600!

But boys' muscles usually are bigger than girls'. One reason is that they use their muscles more in sports, and so their muscles become bigger and harder. Another reason is that when boys reach their teens, their bodies are making special chemicals that help them develop into men. These chemicals also make their muscle cells grow faster and stronger.

WHAT HAPPENS WHEN YOU SMILE?

When you smile everyone can see that you look happy. The muscles in your face can make you look happy or sad, puzzled or mad.

When you smile, one group of muscles goes to work to lift the corners of your mouth and crinkle your eyes. Another group of muscles shapes your face differently when you frown or pout.

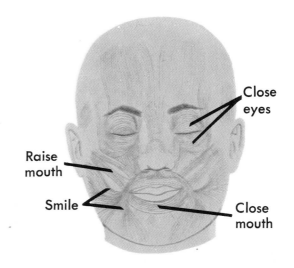

Close eyes

Raise mouth

Smile

Close mouth

WHY DO YOUR ARMS GET TIRED WHEN YOU PLAY BALL TOO LONG?

You use the muscles in your arms to throw a ball. If you play too long your arms feel tired. This is because when you exercise or play you are using up the oxygen that your muscles need to function.

The tired feeling is a signal to rest so that your lungs can get more oxygen into your blood. You breathe deeper and faster even after you have stopped playing ball until enough oxygen has been brought to your muscles to replace what you have used up.

WHO IS "CHARLEY HORSE"?

"Charley Horse" is not a person or an animal. But if you have ever exercised too much and hours later felt that you couldn't move without your muscles aching, you are acquainted with charley horse. This is a term often used for a strain or soreness in your muscles.

Baseball and football players often get charley horse in their legs, especially when they first begin to train for their games. That's when their muscles are not yet used to so much work.

When muscles work too hard at exercise they are not used to, there is not enough blood coming to those muscles to bring the oxygen they need. And there is not enough blood to take away the wastes that have been stored up. These wastes probably cause the soreness which people call charley horse.

WHY DO YOU SHIVER ON A COLD DAY?

On a freezing cold day, sometimes you find yourself shivering. Shivering is your body's way to help make you warm. A shiver is a quick, quivering movement of your muscles. When your muscles move in a shiver, the muscle cells burn more food than usual, and produce more heat in your body. More heat inside you helps to make you warm.

Your Body's Covering—Your Skin

WHY DO YOU NEED SKIN?

How strange you would look walking around with your insides showing! Your skin is your body's covering. But your skin does more than cover your body. Your skin is waterproof and airtight to protect the fluid in which all cells live.

Your skin also helps keep your body at the right temperature. Your body produces heat all the time. It would become much too hot if heat could not escape. Some of this heat escapes when you breathe, but most of it escapes from your skin when you sweat. Sweat is made in glands in your skin.

When you are in the hot sun, more blood passes through the skin because the tiny blood vessels in the skin *dilate*, or get bigger. When more blood is brought to the sweat glands in the skin, these glands become more active. The sweat they produce flows out of the openings or *pores* on the surface of the skin. As the air evaporates or dries up the sweat, heat is given off and is carried away. This makes your skin feel cooler.

When it is very cold, the tiny blood vessels in the skin *constrict*, or get smaller. When this happens, there is little blood at the surface to flow through the sweat glands and they produce only a tiny amount of sweat, or no sweat at all. The blood has flowed to the deeper layers of the skin to prevent its heat from being lost to the cold air.

**Cross section of skin
(greatly enlarged)**

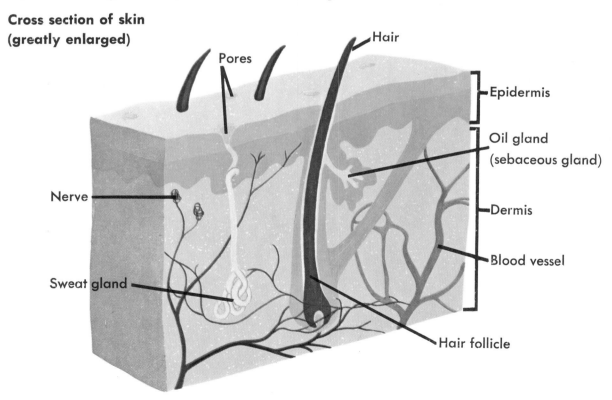

Pores

Hair

Epidermis

Oil gland
(sebaceous gland)

Nerve

Dermis

Blood vessel

Sweat gland

Hair follicle

WHAT MAKES YOUR SKIN WATERPROOF?

All your body's cells live in fluid. Your skin provides a waterproof container so the fluids can't get out, and air can't get in to dry them up.

Your skin, like every part of your body, is made up of cells. You have many layers of skin. The thick outer layer which you can see is called the *epidermis*. It protects the inner layers of the epidermis and the deep inner layer of skin called the *dermis*.

The uppermost layers of the epidermis are composed of dead or dying cells. Many of these come off when you wash or rub your skin. Beneath the top layers new skin cells are produced. Blood vessels, nerves, and sweat and oil glands are in the dermis.

The outer skin must stay oiled to keep it waterproof. The dermis does this job. Glands in the dermis constantly provide oil to keep the outer skin waterproof.

WHY DO PEOPLE HAVE DIFFERENT COLORED SKINS?

Why is the color of your skin brown, or yellow-tan, or pinkish white? The answer lies in the amount of pigment in your skin. You may have heard it said that a person has black skin or white skin or yellow skin. Have you ever seen anyone with skin as white as snow, or as black as the darkest night, or as yellow as a canary? There is no such thing. All skin, no matter what color it is, has the same brown coloring pigment. People who have more pigment have darker skin. People with less have lighter skin.

People with dark skin or light skin—all people—are alike inside.

How much or how little of the brown pigment a person has in his skin has nothing to do with how smart he is, or how nice he is, or how strong he is. It merely determines the color of his skin.

WHY DOESN'T A LITTLE SCRATCH HURT?

You climb over a rough fence and scratch your finger. You rub your hand over the bark of a tree. As you do these things, the cells of your skin's outer layer are constantly rubbing off. There is nothing to worry about. Below the outer layer, more cells are made to take their place. Because the cells of the uppermost layers of the *epidermis* are dead or dying, you don't feel pain when you lose them. All your nerves and blood vessels lie deep in the inner skin, the *dermis*.

HOW DOES A CUT HEAL?

Suppose you cut your finger slightly. Blood flows from tiny blood vessels in your skin. It is almost as if your body called forth a special army to help fight infection and heal the cut. When your finger bleeds, blood helps wash out dirt and germs.

Your finger doesn't bleed for a long time because the blood thickens, or *clots*. Instead of falling in drops, the blood becomes thicker, almost like jelly, and fills the cut. The clot contains small strands, or *fibers*, which form the foun-

dation for the repair work to be done. The clot also keeps out harmful bacteria that might cause an infection. Little by little, the thickened blood hardens until it forms a hard, strong scab.

The cut still has to be closed completely, and repaired. New skin has to be made. The scab acts as a protection while the wound is healing. It falls off when the cut is completely filled in. What is left is a white area, called *scar tissue*. Scar tissue is stronger than skin. Over the scar tissue, new skin grows, and the white mark disappears.

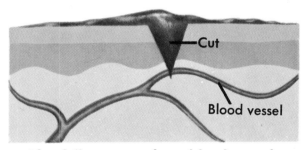

Blood flows out of cut blood vessel.

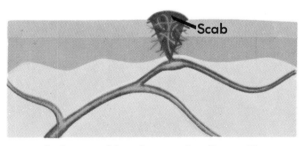

Scab forms, blood vessel still swollen.

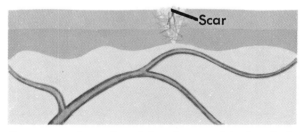

Scar remains after blood vessel is healed.

WHAT ARE FRECKLES?

Do you get a nice even suntan in the summertime? Or do you get a freckle face?

There are certain cells in your skin which manufacture a dark *pigment*, or coloring matter. This pigment is called *melanin*. How much of this dark pigment you have usually depends on how much of it your parents have.

Sunshine helps make this pigment too. When you are in the sun, the cells that manufacture pigment become more active. Your skin may turn an even brown. But sometimes these cells are found only in small areas. When these areas are exposed to the sun, small dark spots appear. These spots are called freckles.

The pigment melanin also protects the deeper layers of the skin from the harmful effects of too much sun.

WHAT ARE WRINKLES?

Your skin fits you perfectly now. But when you were first born, your skin was too big for you. It took six months before your skin really fit your body. Your skin became stretchable, like a rubber band.

When you grow much older, your skin will lose some of its stretch. It will be too big for you again and little folds will develop to take up the slack.

These little folds are wrinkles. You are too young to have any lasting wrinkles. But even now you can wrinkle your forehead. Just open your eyes wide and lift your eyebrows!

WHAT DO YOU HAVE THAT NO ONE ELSE IN THE WORLD HAS?

Look at the tips of your fingers. See the swirls and circles made by the ridges of your skin. They form the special design of your fingertips. No one else in the world has exactly the same design as you have on your fingers. You have your very own special toeprints too!

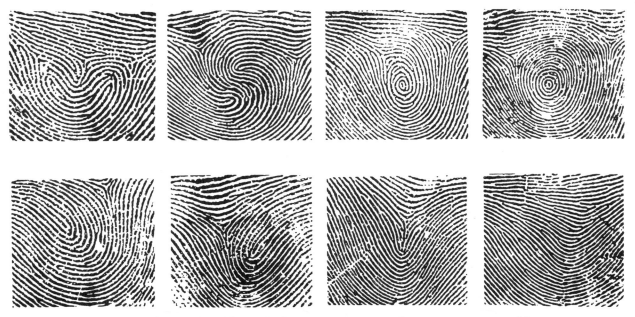

Fingerprint patterns from the files of the F.B.I. No two fingerprints are alike.

Your body grows and changes in many different ways. But the pattern of the ridges on your fingers and toes remain the same all your life.

The police department uses fingerprints to track down criminals. A fingerprint is made by pressing the ends of the fingers on an inked pad and then onto white paper. The police keep fingerprints on file. If they find fingerprints at the scene of a crime, they check them with the fingerprint file.

WHAT IS AN ITCH?

When you suddenly want to scratch your hand or your arm or your foot, it is because you have an itch. An itch may be caused by something inside the body, as when a mosquito bites you and leaves some of its liquid under your skin.

An itch can also be caused by something outside the body like sand rubbing against your skin, or a belt that is too tight. Whatever it is that irritates your skin affects the nerve endings. If the irritation is strong enough, you will feel pain. If the irritation is slight, you will feel a tickle or an itch.

Sometimes you can have an imaginary itch, too. Isn't the back of your head itching right now?

WHY CAN'T YOU HOLD ON TO A PIECE OF ICE?

You pick up a piece of ice. It's cold! You can't hold it very long. What happened when you touched that ice?

In your skin are nerve cells of many different kinds to tell your brain many different things. Some nerve cells respond only to heat. Others react to cold, to pain, to pressure.

When you touched the piece of ice, the nerve cells in your skin that respond to cold went into action. They passed on a message to your spinal cord, and then all the way to your brain, to tell you that what you touched was too cold to hold without hurting your skin.

WHY DO YOU GET GOOSE PIMPLES?

You leave your warm house and go out into the cold air. You may get a prickly feeling on your arms, a feeling that makes you think your hair is "standing on end." You may also see little bumps, called *goose pimples*, on your arms.

When your skin is cold, the tiny muscles attached to each of your hair roots *contract*, or shorten. This causes the fine hairs on your arms to stand up. The hair roots are pushed up too, causing little pimples—goose pimples!

The hair of dogs and cats and other fur-bearing animals stands up when their muscles contract too. But because they have so much more hair, this forms a nice warm "blanket" for them. You need to put on extra clothes in the winter because goose pimples without a hair blanket will not keep you warm.

HOW DOES YOUR HAIR GROW?

Every hair on your body grows from a tiny "root" under your skin. These roots are deep down in the skin in special tubes called *follicles*. At the bottom of each follicle are tiny blood vessels which bring food to the cells. The new cells grow. They push the old cells up along the follicles. And a chemical change turns the old cells into hair.

You can see a cat's hair stand up. The same thing happens to hair in the human body when muscles attached to hair follicles contract.

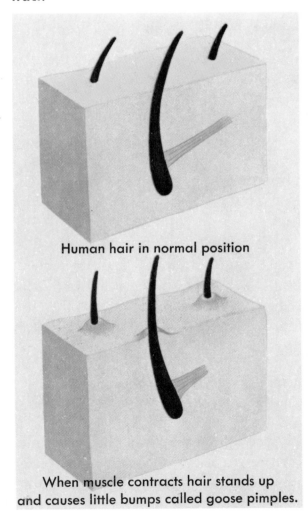

Human hair in normal position

When muscle contracts hair stands up and causes little bumps called goose pimples.

27

HOW FAST DOES THE HAIR ON YOUR HEAD GROW?

In a month, hair grows about three quarters of an inch! Even when you stop growing taller, your hair will still keep growing. It grows faster in the summer than in the winter. It grows faster during the day than at night.

Your hair is very, very strong—as strong as aluminum. If a rope were made out of strands of long hair it could lift an automobile!

WHY DO SOME PEOPLE HAVE STRAIGHT HAIR AND OTHERS CURLY HAIR?

It is the shape of the hair roots that determines whether your hair is curly or straight.

If your hair roots are round, your hair will grow out straight. If your hair roots are flatter, your hair will grow out curly. How straight or how curly your hair is depends on the kind of hair your parents have.

It is possible to have curly hair made straighter and straight hair made curlier. But the shape of the roots can't be changed. As the hair grows out, the part nearest the roots will look as it did at first.

WHY DO SOME PEOPLE HAVE WHITE HAIR?

People with gray or white hair were not born with hair that color. Their hair may once have been flaming red or golden yellow or coal black. What made that color change to gray or white?

The color of your hair comes from a coloring matter called *pigment*. Pigment is made in your hair deep in the scalp. As people get older, the making of pigment slows down. Finally, hair stops making pigment altogether. Hair turns gray and later the gray fades to white.

Perhaps you have seen a person who isn't very old with gray or white hair. This person probably had parents or grandparents whose hair turned gray when they were young, too.

WHY DOESN'T IT HURT WHEN YOUR NAILS AND HAIR ARE CUT?

The hair that grows out of the follicles is no longer made of living cells. There are no nerves in your hair or in your toenails or fingernails.

You feel pain through nerve endings in your skin. Messages of pain are sent to your brain through these nerve endings. And since there are no nerves in your nails or hair, no messages go to your brain. That's why you feel no pain when your nails or hair are cut.

If someone yanks your hair hard, however — *ouch!* That hurts because your hair was pulled from its roots under your skin. There is a tiny muscle and a tiny nerve at the root of each hair. A message of pain was sent from those nerves to your brain.

It hurts, too, when you break a fingernail, but that's because you've exposed the tender skin that the fingernail is meant to protect.

You and Your Senses

HOW DO YOU SEE?

Look at this page. Look across the room. Look out the window. To see different things you have to use your muscles, your brain, and the many parts of your eye.

The muscles of your eyes make it possible for you to move your eyes to see what you want. Light passes through the **clear, transparent** part of your eye

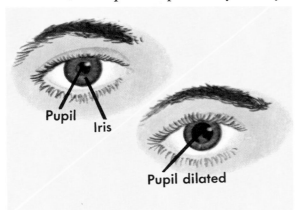

Pupil
Iris
Pupil dilated

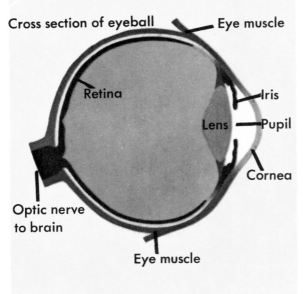

Cross section of eyeball
Eye muscle
Retina
Iris
Lens
Pupil
Cornea
Optic nerve to brain
Eye muscle

called the *cornea*. The cornea covers the colored part of your eye, the *iris*. In the center of the iris is a round hole called the *pupil*. Light passes through the cornea into the pupil. If you are reading these words in very strong light, muscles of the iris make the pupil smaller so that not too much light will enter and hurt your eyes. If you are reading in dim light, these muscles make the hole larger so that more light can come through.

Behind the pupil is the *lens*. If you hold this book close to your eyes, other muscles make the lens small and thick to make the words clear and sharp. If you hold the book far from your eyes, muscles make the lens thin and long to help you see clearly.

The lens throws a picture of what you see on the back of your eyeball—on the *retina*. More than 125 million nerve cells on the retina receive light. The nerve cells carry a message to your brain —and you see!

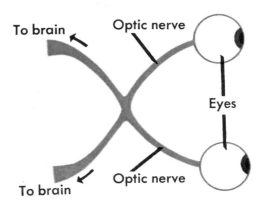

To brain
Optic nerve
Eyes
To brain
Optic nerve
Optic nerve seen from above

The retina contains two different kinds of nerve cells. There are cells shaped like cones, called *cone* cells, which are important for daylight vision. There are cells shaped like rods, called *rod* cells, which are important for seeing in dim light.

Do you know that the picture received on the retina is upside down? But, your brain translates the messages from the nerve cells of your eyes into a picture that is right side up.

HOW IS YOUR EYE LIKE A CAMERA?

Click! You snap the picture of what you see in front of you. Light comes through the lens of your camera. In some cameras you have to adjust the shutter. You set it to open it wide so a lot of light comes in, or you set it to open just a little so less light comes in. The light hits the film in the back of the camera and changes the chemicals which make the light and dark areas on the film's negatives.

Your eyes work something like a camera. The iris is like an automatic shutter (and doesn't need a light exposure meter). It lets the right amount of light into the eye. The light passes through the lens of your eye. The muscles of your lens adjust themselves. You

don't have to turn any knobs or push any buttons. The light strikes the retina at the back of your eye. The light stimulates the cells of the retina, and the nerve endings of the cells send a message to your brain. The message is a picture.

When the film in your camera is used up, you must put in a new roll. Your eyes, however, take picture after picture, every second that they are open. There's no changing film and no waiting for the pictures to be developed.

The newest cameras advertise "electric eyes." But even the most modern camera can't do all the marvelous things your eyes can do.

WHAT HAPPENS WHEN YOU CRY?

"Sticks and stones may break your bones, but names will never hurt you." So the old saying goes. That may be true, but name calling might make you cry!

You are not aware of it, but there are tears in your eyes all the time—even when you are not crying. Your eyes are being washed constantly. They are bathed by a salty fluid made by the tear glands. The amount of fluid is so small that it can drain off into the two small tubes at the corner of your eyes near

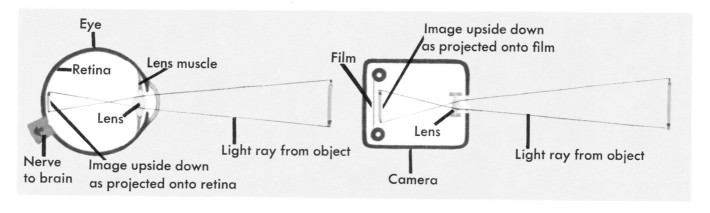

Eye — Retina — Lens muscle — Lens — Nerve to brain — Image upside down as projected onto retina — Light ray from object

Image upside down as projected onto film — Film — Lens — Camera — Light ray from object your nose. Then the fluid flows through tiny openings down into your nose.

But when someone calls you a name or you hurt yourself or you feel weepy and cry, your tear glands make so much of the salty fluid that it can't possibly all flow down into the small tubes. So the tear drops spill from your eyes.

Do you know that only people can cry? Animals never cry. They have tears only to wash their eyes.

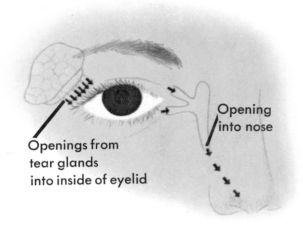

Openings from tear glands into inside of eyelid

Opening into nose

WHAT GOOD ARE EYELASHES AND EYEBROWS?

Eyelashes act as a screen for your eyes. They help keep dust out.

Eyebrows protect your eyes too. When you are hot, sweat forms on your forehead. Your eyebrows stop the sweat from running into your eyes.

CAN NEWBORN BABIES SEE WELL?

If you see a baby boy dressed in pink or a baby girl dressed in blue, don't worry about it. Babies can't tell one color from another, although they can tell the dif-ference between light and dark.

Unless you hold a baby's toy close to his eyes, it will be just a blur to him. But if you bring it close enough, he can probably see it very well. After he's a month old, he has no trouble seeing the world around him.

WHY DO YOU SOMETIMES "SEE STARS" WHEN YOU BUMP YOUR HEAD?

You have probably heard someone say, "I bumped my head so hard I saw stars!" What he thought were stars was really a flash of bright light. A nerve in his eye was playing a trick on him. This nerve is called the *optic* nerve. A hard bump on the head stimulates the optic nerve. The nerve sends a message to the brain, which translates the message as a burst of light. Most people describe this as "seeing stars."

HOW IS YOUR SKIN LIKE A REPORTER?

The many kinds of nerve cells in your skin give you your sense of touch and report to your brain such feelings as hot or cold, soft or hard, smooth or rough. They also report sensations of pain and pressure, tickle and itch.

Your skin acts as a bodyguard as well as a reporter. Through nerve endings in your skin you know when to stay away from something that will hurt you. If you touch a hot stove by accident, the nerve endings in the skin of your fingers send a message to your brain to tell you not to do it again.

HOW DO YOU TASTE?

You can't taste anything if it is dry. As soon as a piece of food gets on your tongue, it becomes wet. Around and under your tongue are three glands which make a liquid called *saliva*. Saliva flows into your mouth and wets your food so you can taste it.

Stick out your tongue. Can you see little bumps on it? Inside those bumps are many cells which form *taste buds*. You have four kinds of taste buds on your tongue, each kind grouped in a different place. On one place on your tongue you taste bitter foods. On another place you taste salty things. You taste sour foods someplace else on your tongue and sweet foods at still another.

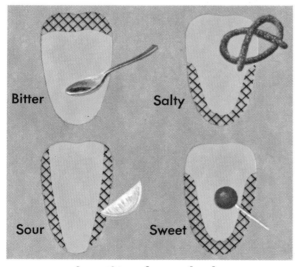

Location of taste buds

Your taste buds send a message to your brain that a taste is bitter or salty or sour or sweet or a mixture of these flavors.

Suppose you eat a piece of strong-smelling cheese. You don't taste the cheese with your tongue alone. You taste it by smelling it too!

WHY IS A LOLLYPOP GOOD TO LICK?

The back of your tongue is where you taste bitter foods. At the side you taste sour foods. At the front you taste sweet foods. That's why the lollypop is so good to lick. The sweet buds are right at the tip of your tongue!

HOW WELL CAN YOU SMELL?

A dog can tell if his master is coming down the street even if he can't see him. A dog knows his master's special smell. A dog's special sense of smell is much keener than yours. Yet dogs and cats and other animals can't smell as many different odors as you can.

The part of your nose that you see is not the part you smell with. You smell by means of special nerve cells deep inside your nose, very near the brain.

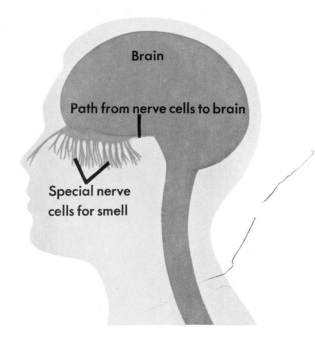

CAN YOU TASTE CHOCOLATE ICE CREAM WITH YOUR NOSE?

You taste the sweetness of ice cream with the taste buds at the tip of your tongue. But the flavor of the chocolate is a job for your sense of smell.

Chocolate has a distinct odor. What makes this smell? It is the chocolate releasing tiny particles of *vapor*, or gas. Just as you can't taste anything if your mouth is dry, you can't smell anything if the inside of your nose is dry. The particles of vapor, released by the chocolate, are moistened inside your nose by a fluid called *mucus*. Nerve cells inside your nose are stimulated by the moistened particles.

While your tongue is reporting to your brain that you're eating something sweet and creamy, the nerve cells in your nose are reporting that it's also something chocolatey. Your brain puts two and two together and you say, "*Mmmmn!* Chocolate ice cream!"

WHY DOESN'T FOOD TASTE AS GOOD WHEN YOU HAVE A COLD?

Most of the food you *taste*, you really *smell*, too. When you have a cold, your taste buds continue to work well. But, when your nose is stuffed, the flavor can't get through to that part of your nose where the sense-of-smell cells are located. So the food seems tasteless.

WHY ARE THE SMELLS OF FOOD SO STRONG WHEN YOU FIRST SMELL THEM?

Suppose your mother is boiling cabbage. "What a smell! How can you stand it?" you might say. But your mother doesn't mind. She's been in the kitchen for a while, and her smell nerves have tired of the same odor. The nerve cells have stopped sending reports of smelly cabbage to her brain. This is "getting used to" a particular smell. After a few minutes in the kitchen, your nerve cells tire of the cabbage smell, too, and you don't notice it either.

WHY DO YOU SNIFF TO SMELL A FLOWER?

The nerve cells which enable you to tell one smell from another are located high up at the back of your nose, above the passageway where you breathe. By sniffing, you carry the delicate odor of the flower up to where these smell nerve cells can recognize the flower's special fragrance.

If you hold your nose, you block the breathing passageway and the odor of the flower or anything else can't reach the sense-of-smell nerve cells.

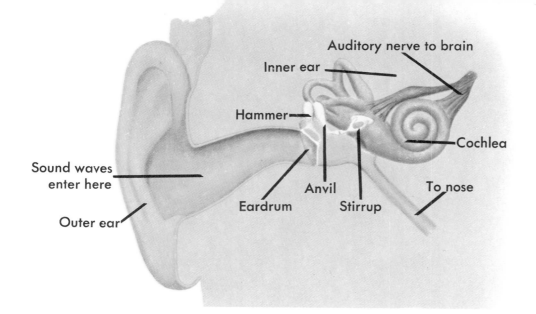

Auditory nerve to brain

Inner ear

Hammer

Cochlea

Sound waves enter here

Anvil

To nose

Eardrum

Stirrup

Outer ear

HOW DO YOU HEAR?

The part of your ear that you see is not the most necessary part for hearing. The really important parts for hearing are inside your head.

Make a growling sound. You've just set up quivering movements in the air—*vibrations*. The part of the ear that you can see collects the vibrating waves of sound. Then the sound waves travel to your *eardrum*, a thin, taut membrane. The vibrations make the eardrum quiver, and three tiny bones inside the eardrum move with each vibration. From there, the vibrations travel to a tube which looks like a snail shell. Inside this tube, called the *cochlea*, are thousands of nerve cells. They are arranged in order, like the keys of a xylophone, with the low notes at one end, the high notes at the other. The tube is filled with fluid. The vibrating waves of sound now cause the fluid to vibrate. The fluid presses on the nerve cells that are at the "low note" end. And these sensitive nerve cells pass on the message of your growl to the hearing center in your brain.

CAN YOU FEEL YOUR VOICE?

Put your fingers on your throat and growl. Do you feel a quivering, buzzing sensation on your fingers? The buzzing came from the "voice box" or *larynx* inside your throat.

Inside the larynx are two vocal cords. When you growled, air passed between the vocal cords and made them vibrate, causing the sound of growling.

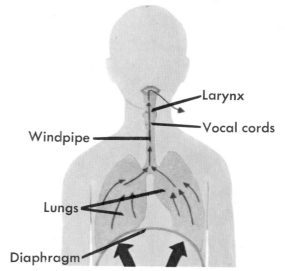

Larynx

Vocal cords

Windpipe

Lungs

Diaphragm

Large arrows show pressure of the diaphragm against the lungs. When the air is pushed up through the larynx, it reaches the vocal cords. The cords vibrate and sound is produced.

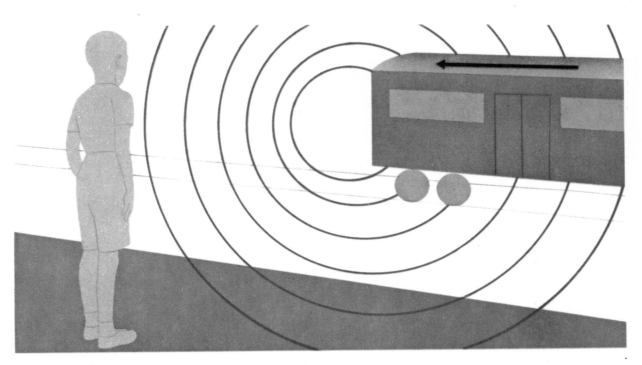

HOW CAN YOU TELL FROM WHICH DIRECTION A TRAIN IS COMING?

You are standing at a train station. You hear the roar of the train and without looking you can tell whether it's coming from your right or your left. The vibrating waves of sound strike the ear closer to the train more directly and with more intensity than they do the other ear.

DO PEOPLE WHO CAN WIGGLE THEIR EARS HEAR BETTER?

A rabbit sits in the garden, listening intently for every sound. His ears quiver slightly. A rabbit's ears are large and they can collect sound waves and guide them inside. The muscles in a rabbit's ears are developed so that he can turn his ears in different directions to hear better.

To hear better, you have to turn your head. You can't turn your ears like a rabbit. You have muscles in your ears but you can't move them—unless you are one of the few people who can wiggle his ears. People who wiggle their ears can make others laugh—but they can't hear any better than anyone else.

WHICH OF YOUR SENSES HELPS YOU WHEN YOU CLIMB A TREE?

Besides your senses of sight, smell, taste, sound, and touch, you have still another sense that helps you when you want to climb a tree.

There are sensory nerve endings in your muscles, joints, and tendons that give you your "muscle sense."

How far from the ground do you have to jump to reach that heavy branch? Can one hand support your weight while you reach with the other for the next higher branch?

Your muscle sense answers these questions. Your muscles report what they are doing to your brain. Your brain, in turn, helps your muscles know what to do. Your muscle sense helped you when you were learning how to play ball and how to swim.

Your Giant Message Center—
Your Brain and Nervous System

WHAT GOES ON INSIDE YOUR BRAIN?

Everything! Everything you do, everything you think about, every movement your body makes—all these things are possible because your marvelous brain controls every one of your actions and thoughts.

You remember that two and two are four, you turn off a light switch, you think about someone you met last week, you read these words, you laugh at something funny, you feel pity and love for a wounded pet—the list of things you can do because of your brain would fill many, many pages.

Your brain makes it possible for you to think and dream and plan and remember. You walk and talk, write and read, see and hear, and taste and laugh and cry because of your brain. Your brain controls your breathing and the beating of your heart. Your brain keeps you alive.

There is nothing in the world as remarkable as the human brain.

WHAT ARE THE THREE MAIN PARTS OF YOUR BRAIN?

The biggest part of your brain is the thinking part called the *cerebrum*. This

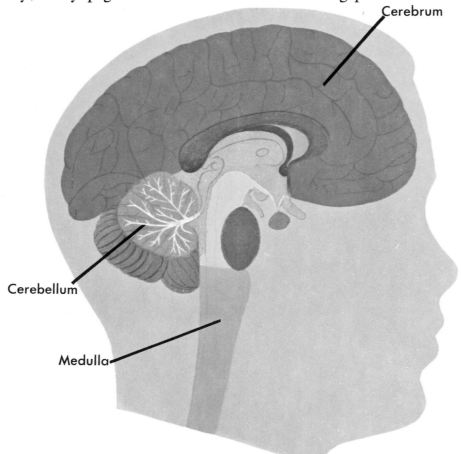

Cerebrum

Cerebellum

Medulla

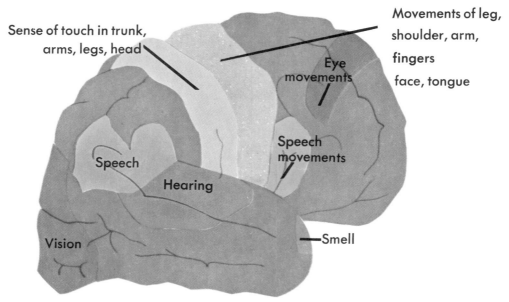

Right half of cerebrum (outside) showing location of special areas.

part makes it possible for you to read a book and think about what you read. It's this part that receives messages from the nerves that enable you to smell, taste, feel, see, and hear. You use this part of your brain to wish and hope and dream and plan. It's this part of your brain that makes decisions and choices. Everything you've ever learned or will learn is stored in the cerebrum.

The cerebrum also sends messages to the muscles when you decide to move.

These messages have to go through a part of your brain called the *cerebellum*. This part of your brain is where the right orders are given to your muscles to make them work together properly and to carry out the messages from the thinking part of your brain. The cerebellum is the size of a small rubber ball. It couldn't work without the thinking part of your brain.

The third important part of your brain is the *medulla*. The medulla is in charge of important nerves which control muscles you never have to think about. The medulla gives the orders to the muscles that are necessary to keep your body working while you are thinking about other things.

WHAT DOES THE LARGEST PART OF YOUR BRAIN LOOK LIKE?

The *cerebrum* is the largest part of your brain, occupying the whole top. It has a thin, outer layer called the *cerebral cortex*. This outer layer is packed with billions of nerve cells—so many nerve cells that the cortex has to fold over itself to fit inside the bones of your skull. The folds make this part of the brain look wrinkled, like the inside of a walnut.

HOW DO YOU REMEMBER WHAT YOU DID YESTERDAY?

Did it rain? Was the sun shining? Was it a happy or a sad day for you? To think

38

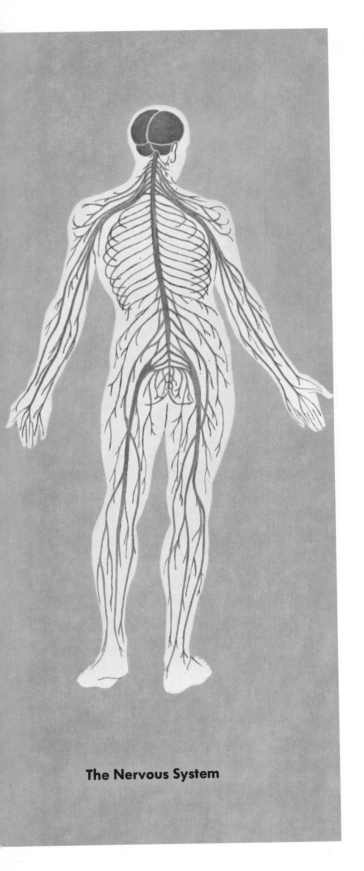

The Nervous System

about yesterday and to remember what happened, you use one of the three main parts of your brain—the thinking part, the *cerebrum*.

Perhaps you'd like to tell someone what you did yesterday. This information is stored in the cerebrum. It's this part of your brain that enables you to remember what you did and to speak the words that describe what happened.

WHAT KEEPS YOUR HEART BEATING?

Your heart beats all by itself. But the part of your brain called the *medulla* determines how fast and how strong your heart beats.

The medulla also controls the muscles of your stomach and your lungs, night and day. You never have to think: "Heart, pump fast!" or Lungs, breathe!"

HOW DOES YOUR BRAIN RECEIVE AND SEND MESSAGES?

The brain might be called the headquarters of a giant message system. The brain receives messages from every part of your body by way of a huge network of nerves. It sorts out the information in these messages and it replies with messages of its own to tell the different parts of the body what action to take.

Suppose you are sitting down and you decide to stand up. Sounds simple, but in order to do it, your brain must send messages to 200 pairs of muscles. Your muscles go into action in just the right

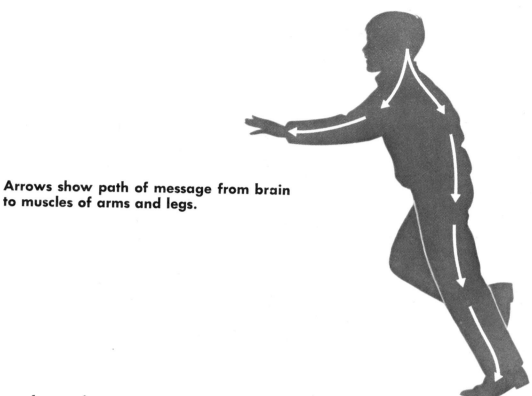

Arrows show path of message from brain to muscles of arms and legs.

order so that you can get up and stand on your two feet.

Some nerve cells are longer than any other cells of your body. One nerve cell may stretch from your brain to almost the end of your spinal cord. Another nerve cell reaches from there right down to your foot. Each nerve cell has the remarkable ability to send a slight charge of electricity to the cell next to it. That's how messages go to and from your brain. Some messages travel at a speed of two hundred miles an hour!

HOW DOES YOUR BRAIN HELP YOU PLAY TAG?

In a game of tag you do many things. You run, you reach out your hand to tag a player, you touch him, you shout: "You're it!" and then you start to run again.

The thinking part of your brain decides to play tag. It sends a message to the action part of your brain. The action part signals the muscles you need to run in a certain direction, to tag your friend, and to run again so you won't be tagged.

On the way, these signals pass through a part of your brain that acts as a control center. Here all the signals are organized so that you move the right muscles at the right time with the right strength.

How long does it take from the time you decide to play until you're actually playing? Your brain works fast! It takes your brain only a fraction of a second to start the many muscles in your arms and legs moving in perfect order.

WHY DO YOU DROP A HOT POTATO?

You drop a hot potato *before* you even feel the pain that comes from burning your hand. As soon as you touched the potato, nerves speedily sent a message— *too hot!* This special danger message reached the spinal cord before it reached the brain. Immediately, motor nerves in

the spinal cord answered the message by making you spread out your fingers so you would drop the potato. You didn't even have to think about spreading out your fingers. This kind of movement is called a *reflex action.*

Then the message went from your spinal cord to your brain. Your brain made you aware that the potato was too hot to touch—that touching it caused you pain. Your brain made you decide to use a towel or a potholder to protect your hand from being burned when you picked up the hot potato again.

If someone flashes a light in your eyes, you will blink. If you sniff pepper, you will sneeze. If someone shouts "Boo" at you, you will jump.

The muscles that made you blink, sneeze or jump went to work before the brain knew what was happening. Blinking, sneezing, and jumping are other examples of reflex actions.

If you go from a dark room into a bright room, another reflex action takes place. The pupils of your eyes change size. In a dark room, the pupils become larger to let in more light. They become smaller when you go into a bright room. Muscles of the eye make these changes without sending messages to your brain.

Another kind of reflex is the *conditioned reflex.* When a dish of food is set before a dog, its mouth begins to water— that is, saliva begins to flow. If you rang a bell at the same time you placed the dog's food in front of him, and you did this for a number of days, the dog's mouth would begin to water just at the sound of the bell. The dog wouldn't need to see or smell his food. This is an example of a conditioned reflex.

People have conditioned reflexes too. Suppose your mother always rang a bell to let you know that supper was on the table. If you were hungry, you wouldn't need to see the food. Your mouth would begin to water at the sound of the supper bell.

WHY DOES THE DOCTOR TAP YOUR KNEE?

The doctor taps your knee just below your kneecap. Instantly your foot kicks forward. This shows the doctor that your reflexes are in good working order.

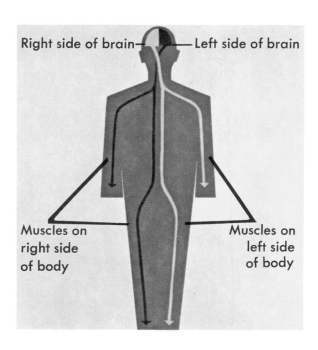

Right side of brain — Left side of brain

Muscles on right side of body

Muscles on left side of body

WHY ARE SOME PEOPLE LEFT-HANDED?

Whether you write with your left hand or your right—or equally well with both depends upon the development of your brain. Some brains develop more on one side than on the other.

Do you know that the left side of your brain controls the muscles on the right side of your body and that the right side of your brain controls the muscles on the left side of your body?

If the left side of your brain is more developed than the right side, you are right-handed. If the right side of the brain is more developed than the left, you are left-handed. If your brain is developed equally on both sides, you are *ambidextrous*. That means you can use your right or your left hand to play ball or to write. Most people are right-handed. Are you?

DO SMARTER PEOPLE HAVE BIGGER BRAINS?

When you were three years old, your brain had reached two-thirds of its full size. It will continue to grow until you are about 20 years old. At that time it will weigh about three pounds.

It's not the size of the brain that makes one person smart and another a fool. It's the way the brain develops. The brains of brilliant men seldom seem to differ in weight or size from those of stupid men.

IS AN IBM MACHINE SMARTER THAN YOUR BRAIN?

Man has planned and invented and built complicated machines called computers to solve complicated problems. It would take a man his whole lifetime to solve a problem that a computer can solve in minutes.

That does not mean, however, that a computer is smarter than man. After all, it is man's brain that designed the computer in the first place. It is man's brain that makes it possible for him to know how the computer works. Yet no man, no scientist, has yet answered all the questions that have been raised about our most important computer—the human brain.

The Food You Eat

WHY DO YOU EAT?

You eat because it's fun to eat, especially when you're hungry. You usually feel hungry at certain times because you're used to eating at those times.

But you really eat to feed your cells so that your body can grow healthy and strong. You eat so you can have the energy to play and to work.

WHY DO YOU NEED WATER?

Your body needs water as well as food. No one can stay alive for more than a few days without water. A large part of your body is made up of water. Your cells contain water. So does your blood.

When the blood passes through the kidneys, many of the wastes of the body are dissolved in water and removed in liquid form. This means that you lose a lot of water in order to get rid of the wastes and keep your blood clean.

You also lose water as you breathe and as you sweat.

Water is found in most of the foods you eat and in the milk you drink. You should also drink a few glasses of water each day to help replace the water your body loses.

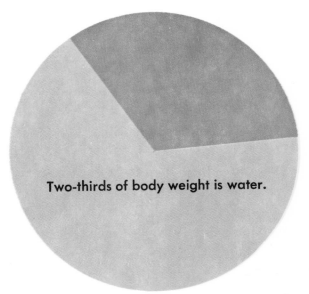

Two-thirds of body weight is water.

The circle represents your body weight. The light green area shows how much of the body weight is water.

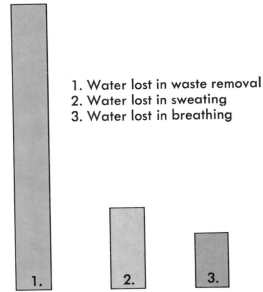

1. Water lost in waste removal
2. Water lost in sweating
3. Water lost in breathing

1.   2.   3.

The columns above show how much more water is lost by waste removal than by sweating or breathing.

43

WHY DOES YOUR STOMACH RUMBLE WHEN YOU'RE HUNGRY?

When you eat, food goes into your stomach. Glands in your stomach make a fluid called *gastric juice*. Gastric juice contains special chemicals called *enzymes*. Enzymes break down the food very quickly into particles tiny enough to enter the cells.

You usually have your breakfast, lunch, and supper at the same time each day. Your stomach makes gastric juice on a regular schedule. With nothing in your stomach to absorb this juice, it can sometimes get noisy—almost as if it were saying, "Hey, when do we eat?"

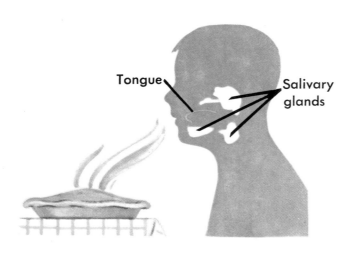

Tongue — Salivary glands

WHAT HAPPENS WHEN YOU SMELL GOOD FOOD?

A sweet spicy smell comes from the kitchen. You sniff. *Mmmm*—apple pie! You can hardly wait for dinner.

Then a strange thing happens. You feel the inside of your mouth becoming wet. What you feel is *saliva*. Saliva enters your mouth from glands around your tongue. Your salivary glands are constantly keeping your mouth moist. But they become more active when you eat or smell good food. Your tongue, teeth, and saliva work together to prepare food for the first part of digestion.

You can make your mouth "water" without seeing or smelling good food. Wait until you're very hungry. Then think of your favorite food. You'll find your mouth will begin to water.

WHAT HAPPENED TO THE BREAKFAST YOU ATE THIS MORNING?

Suppose you had orange juice, a bowl of cereal, a piece of toast with butter and jam, and a glass of milk for breakfast this morning. When you ate everything, you may have said, "I'm finished!"

But your body wasn't. It was just beginning its work. Your breakfast had to be changed into food for your cells. This process is called *digestion*.

A lot had to be done with that breakfast. Solid food had to be changed into almost liquid form and broken down into tiny particles called *molecules*. The molecules had to be absorbed into the bloodstream and carried to all your body's cells.

Many parts of your body work to digest your food—your tongue, teeth, and the many parts that make up your *digestive system*.

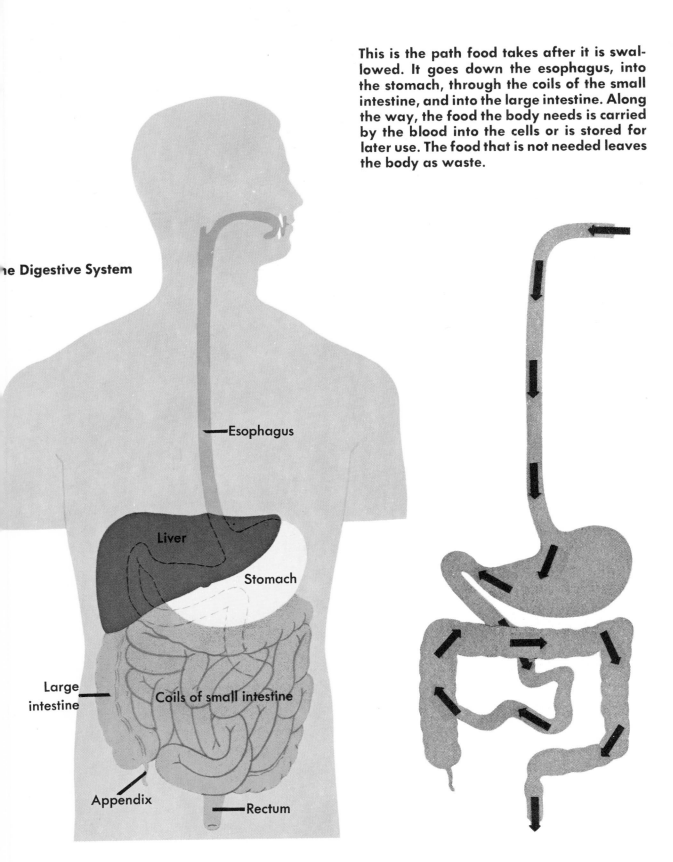

This is the path food takes after it is swallowed. It goes down the esophagus, into the stomach, through the coils of the small intestine, and into the large intestine. Along the way, the food the body needs is carried by the blood into the cells or is stored for later use. The food that is not needed leaves the body as waste.

The Digestive System

Esophagus

Liver

Stomach

Large intestine

Coils of small intestine

Appendix

Rectum

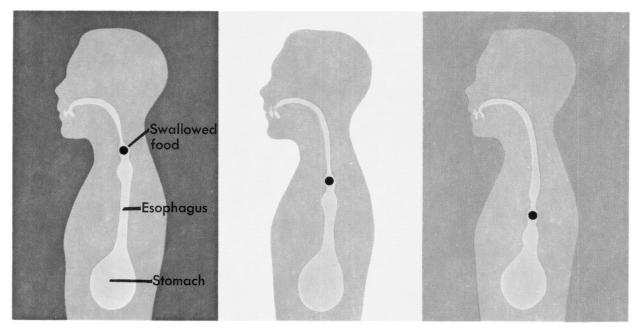

Food being pushed down into the stomach by the muscles of the esophagus

WHAT HAPPENS TO FOOD WHEN IT'S IN YOUR MOUTH?

You cut a piece of steak and place it on your tongue. Your tongue moves it between your teeth. As you chew, your teeth tear and chop and crush it. Saliva from your mouth moistens the steak so you can swallow it easily.

If you've ever had a stomach ache, it might have been because you didn't chew your food well enough and your stomach had to work extra hard to digest it.

When you chew some foods, like bread or potatoes, the saliva does more than help you swallow.

The saliva begins to change starchy food into a form that your body can use. This is the first step in digesting bread or potatoes or other starchy foods.

WHERE DOES YOUR FOOD GO AFTER YOU SWALLOW IT?

After you swallow your food, it goes down the *esophagus*, a long tube at the back of your throat that leads to your stomach. Ring-shaped muscles in this tube push the food down—one muscle after another until it reaches your stomach.

Your stomach is like a stretchable bag lined with muscles. These muscles can stretch to hold a big dinner. The stomach wall is lined with glands that make *gastric juice*. When the food you eat reaches your stomach, the gastric juice continues the job of breaking down the food into the tiniest particles.

When this part of digestion is finished, the food is in a partly liquid form. It then passes, a little at a time, into a long tube called the *small intestine*. The small intestine is not really as small as its name suggests. In fact, it is so long it has to be coiled to fit in your body. Muscles of the small intestine finish pushing the food along until it is finally ready to be used by your cells.

CAN YOU SWALLOW STANDING ON YOUR HEAD?

Try it and see. Ask a friend to help you stand on your head. But be sure there's a wall to lean on. Ask him to give you a glass of water. Try to drink some. You'll find that you can!

Swallowing is a job for muscles over which you have no control. As soon as the water reaches the very back of your mouth, you begin to swallow without even thinking about it.

In the wall of the long tube at the back of your throat that leads to your stomach are little ring-shaped muscles. Water doesn't just drop down—*plink*—into your stomach when you drink. The muscles, one after another, push the water through until it reaches your stomach—even if you are standing on your head.

This isn't the most comfortable way to drink a glass of water, but it proves that food and water do not just fall into your stomach after you swallow them. They are pushed down by the muscles of the esophagus.

WHERE ARE THE DIFFERENT KINDS OF FOOD YOU EAT DIGESTED?

The different foods you eat are digested in different parts of your body. For example, meat is only partly digested in the stomach. The last stage takes place in the small intestine. Fatty foods, such as butter, are digested only in the small intestine.

The digestion of some foods, such as bread, cake, and potatoes, starts in the mouth where they are chemically changed by the saliva. But this is only the first step. The main job of digestion of these foods, too, takes place in the small intestine.

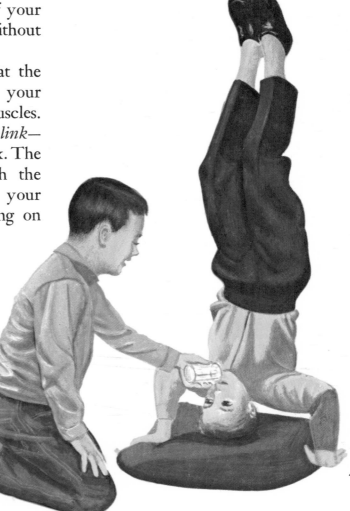

HOW DO THE CELLS OF YOUR BODY GET THE FOOD THEY NEED?

All along the lining of the coiled intestine are millions of tiny, almost hairlike tubes called *villi*. The villi make a larger surface inside the intestine for the digested food to pass through on its way to the bloodstream.

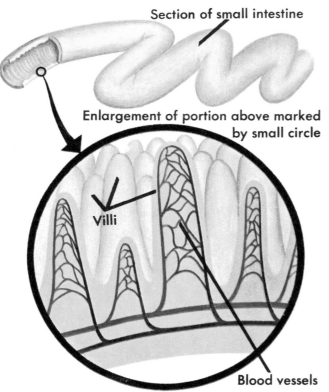

Section of small intestine

Enlargement of portion above marked by small circle

Villi

Blood vessels

Your blood flows through or near every part of your body. Every cell in your body that needs food gets it from the blood as it flows past.

The food your body doesn't need immediately is stored for later use. Blood carries this extra food to your *liver*. Extra food is also stored in layers of fat under your skin. If any part of your body needs this food, the blood supplies it from these storehouses.

WHAT HAPPENS TO THE FOOD YOUR BODY DOESN'T NEED?

The food your body can't use is called *waste material*. It travels from your small intestine into a wider tube, the *large intestine*. The cells of the large intestine take in some of the water from the liquid digested matter. This water goes back into the bloodstream. Solid waste material stays in the large intestine for about twelve hours. Then it is ready to leave the body.

HOW LONG DOES IT TAKE TO DIGEST A MEAL?

Your body is working all the time to digest your food. You eat every four hours or so during the day, but the complete job of digestion takes about twenty-four hours. It starts when your mouth waters at the sight or smell of good food. It ends when your body gets rid of the materials your cells can't use.

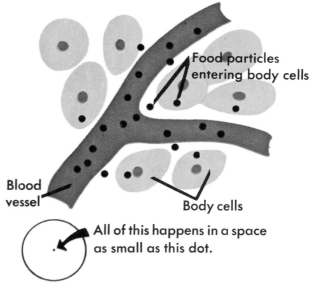

Food particles entering body cells

Blood vessel

Body cells

All of this happens in a space as small as this dot.

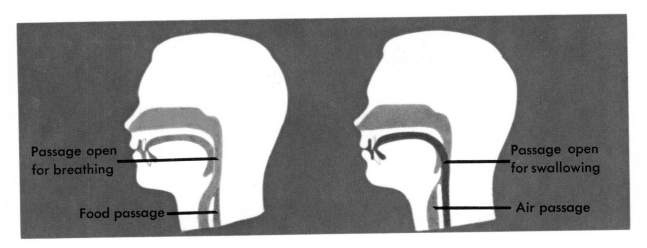

Passage open for breathing

Food passage

Passage open for swallowing

Air passage

WHAT HAPPENS WHEN FOOD GOES DOWN THE WRONG WAY?

At the back of your mouth are several openings. One is a passage for food. Another is a passage for air, called the *windpipe*. When you swallow your food, the windpipe closes and food goes down the food passage.

But suppose you have important news that you just have to tell at the same time you're chewing your food. That's when a bit of food or a sip of drink might get into the windpipe instead of the foodpipe—and you begin to cough. You can't stop coughing until the food is pushed out of the windpipe.

WHY DO YOU FEEL SLEEPY AFTER A BIG MEAL?

Do you remember what you had for Thanksgiving dinner? Perhaps you had turkey and stuffing and sweet potatoes and pie. You probably ate a lot and didn't feel like running around after dinner. You probably felt as stuffed as the turkey itself, and a little sleepy.

Just think of the work your stomach and intestine had to do with all that food! When you eat a big meal, your stomach has to work very hard, getting the food ready for your cells to use.

After a big meal, some of the blood supply from your brain goes to your stomach and intestine to help you digest all that food. Without a good supply of blood in your brain, you feel sleepy.

WHY SHOULDN'T YOU SWIM RIGHT AFTER YOU EAT?

The main job for your body right after you eat is to make sure the food is digested properly. The parts of your body that work hard digesting your food need blood. At this time, there is not enough blood to supply the muscles you use when you swim. Without a full, rich supply of blood in your muscles, you may get a muscle cramp in your legs while swimming. That's why it is a good idea to wait a while before swimming— to let the blood supply build up again in your leg muscles.

Carbohydrates

Fats

Protein

Minerals

WHAT KINDS OF FOOD DOES YOUR BODY NEED?

The cells of your body need food to make energy. They need food to make new cells and to repair cells that wear out or are scraped away.

The food you eat is broken down into the materials your body needs.

You need *carbohydrates* for energy. Some foods that will give you plenty of pep are potatoes, fruits, honey, cereal, corn, peas, and beans.

You need *fats* for energy too. Some fats are stored in your body for later use. Milk, butter, meat, and ice cream are some foods which provide the fats you need.

You need *protein* for making and repairing cells. Milk, eggs, cheese, beans, chicken, fish, meats, and nuts give you protein.

Your body also needs *minerals* for strong teeth and bones. One such mineral is iron. But don't eat nails. Eat liver and green vegetables and drink milk to get the minerals you need.

Vitamins come in pills, of course, but they are also found in many foods. You need vitamins for energy and for keeping healthy.

Breathing In, Breathing Out

WHAT HAPPENS WHEN YOU BREATHE?

Each time you breathe in, *oxygen* goes into your lungs. Each time you breathe out, a gas called *carbon dioxide* goes out of your lungs.

This is how it happens: Air (which contains oxygen) enters your body through your nose. Air is filled with tiny bits of dust and germs. Fine hairs inside your nose and a sticky liquid, called *mucus*, keep most of the dust and germs from going into your lungs.

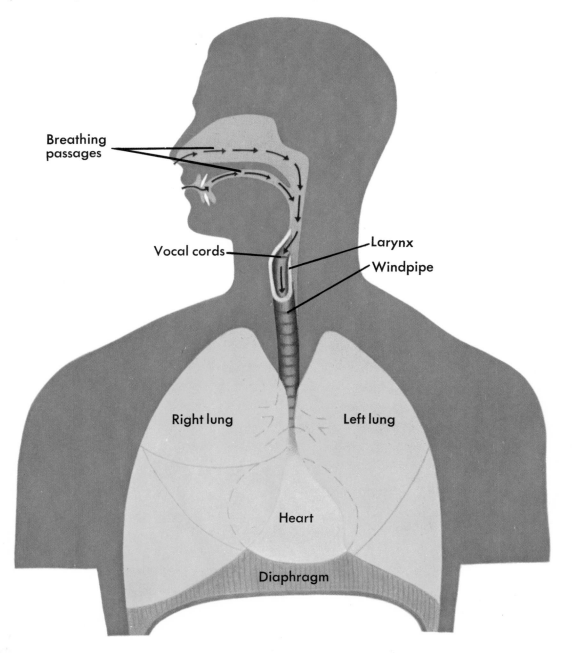

Breathing passages

Vocal cords

Larynx

Windpipe

Right lung

Left lung

Heart

Diaphragm

The air you breathe is warmed by blood vessels that line the inside of your nose. The warmed, cleaned air passes into the long windpipe in your throat. The windpipe branches into two pipes —one for each of your two lungs. These two pipes divide into smaller and narrower pipes inside your lungs. The smallest pipes lead to millions of tiny *air sacs*. Here, in the air sacs of your lungs, a most important exchange takes place.

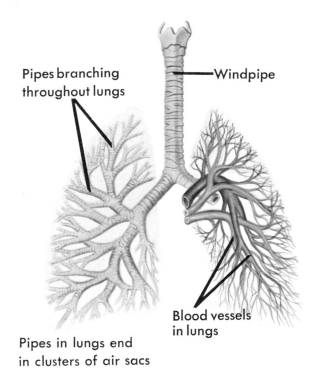

Pipes branching throughout lungs

Windpipe

Blood vessels in lungs

Pipes in lungs end in clusters of air sacs

Surrounding the air sacs are tiny blood vessels. The oxygen you have breathed in passes through the air sacs *into* these blood vessels and is carried by the blood to the cells. At the same time, the carbon dioxide in the blood passes *from* these tiny blood vessels into the air sacs of the lungs.

When you exhale, you breathe out this carbon dioxide. When you inhale, you breathe in air that contains the fresh oxygen your cells need.

It is not the lungs themselves that pump in the oxygen and pump out the carbon dioxide. It is the muscles between your ribs, and a curved muscle under your lungs, called the *diaphragm* that do this job. These muscles make your lungs inflate and deflate like balloons by changing the size of your *rib*

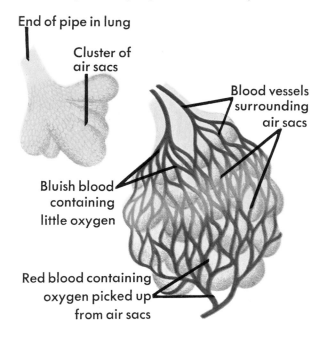

End of pipe in lung

Cluster of air sacs

Blood vessels surrounding air sacs

Bluish blood containing little oxygen

Red blood containing oxygen picked up from air sacs

cage. When the rib cage is larger, the lungs can fill up with air. When it is smaller, the carbon dioxide is forced out.

WHY DO YOU HAVE TO BREATHE TO STAY ALIVE?

When you breathe in, you draw air into your lungs. In the air is a gas called oxy-

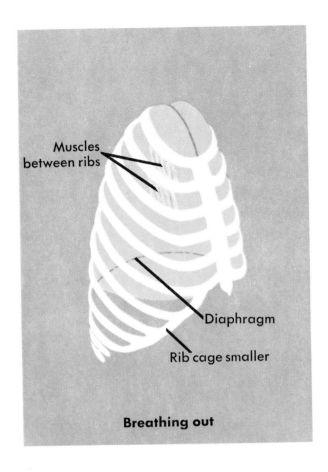

Muscles between ribs

Diaphragm

Rib cage smaller

Breathing out

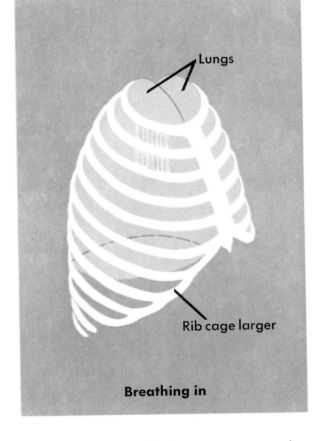

Lungs

Rib cage larger

Breathing in

gen. Without oxygen you cannot stay alive.

Your blood carries food to your cells but the cells cannot make use of this food without oxygen. Oxygen changes the food into energy that the cells can use. Your cells need energy to move the muscles of your body, to send messages along the nerves, and to make new cells.

There is another reason why your body needs oxygen.

When the oxygen you breathe changes the food you eat into energy, heat is given off. That is why you usually feel warm after you have eaten a heavy meal. This heat helps keep the inside of your body warm even if the outside temperature falls to zero. You

cannot stay alive if the temperature inside your body falls too low.

HOW FAST DO YOU BREATHE?

Right now you are breathing about 18 times a minute. If you happen to be reading this page and jumping up and down at the same time, you are breathing much faster.

When you sit quietly you usually breathe through your nose. But when you race around or play actively, you find yourself breathing quickly through your mouth because you can take in more air that way. You also take much deeper breaths. That's how your blood gets the extra oxygen it needs when you use up so much energy quickly.

WHY DO YOU HICCUP?

No one knows exactly why. You hiccup when certain nerves are over-stimulated. These nerves lead to the *diaphragm*, a muscle that helps to work the pumping of your lungs. No one knows what causes these nerves to react in this way.

How can you stop hiccups? One way is to breathe into a paper bag. When you do this, you are breathing in your own breath. You breathe in more carbon dioxide which seems to quiet the over-stimulated nerves, and the hiccups stop.

Some people say a good way to cure hiccups is to stand on your head or to have someone scare you by saying "BOO!"

But usually, if you do nothing at all to stop your hiccups, chances are they will probably go away by themselves.

WHY DO YOU SNEEZE?

Kachoo! You sneeze once—maybe twice. Usually you sneeze to get rid of an irritation in the air passage in your nose. Sneezing is a *reflex* action.

As soon as this troublesome something gets into your breathing passage, a message goes to your brain: "Get rid of it!" The brain than sends another message to the breathing muscles of your ribs and diaphragm. And out goes the bothersome annoyance—with a sneeze!

CAN YOU STOP YOURSELF FROM SNEEZING?

You can't usually stop a first sneeze. But you can do something about the second or third sneeze. When you feel your nose tickle—a sign that another sneeze is on its way—bite your lip until it hurts a little. The pain signals which your nerves send to your brain are more urgent than the signals sent from your nose. And so the second sneeze may be blocked—or at least you won't sneeze as hard.

WHY CAN'T YOU BREATHE UNDER WATER?

You breathe in oxygen from the air. There is oxygen in water, too, but you can't take the oxygen from the water. If you tried to breathe under water, your lungs would quickly fill up with water and you wouldn't be able to breathe at all.

If you were a fish or a crab, you could breathe under water but you couldn't breathe on land. Fish and other sea animals have organs called *gills* which enable them to take oxygen from the water. But if a fish is taken out of the water, its gills dry out and it can't breathe.

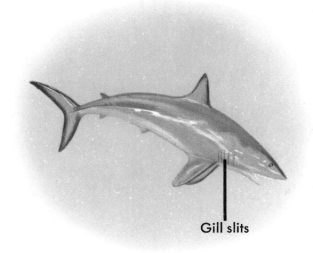

Gill slits

WHY CAN'T YOU HOLD YOUR BREATH FOR MORE THAN THREE MINUTES?

When you stop breathing you begin to store up the gas, carbon dioxide. An increase of carbon dioxide in the blood stimulates the part of your brain that controls breathing and soon you are forced to breathe again, no matter how hard you try to hold your breath.

Have you ever seen a young child having a temper tantrum? He holds his breath until it may look as if he'll never breathe again. But there is no need to worry. The breathing centers of the brain are so sensitive to too much carbon dioxide that the child *must* breathe again.

You can't hold your breath for more than a few minutes. But with special training some people can. For instance, a pearl diver, who has to stay under water to do his job, is taught how to hold his breath for a longer time.

Your Amazing Pump—Your Heart

HOW IS YOUR HEART LIKE A POWERFUL PUMP?

Everytime your heart beats, it pumps. Your heart constantly pumps blood through your blood vessels to every part of your body.

In fact, your heart is really two pumps! One pump receives the bluish-red blood which has just delivered food and oxygen to the body's cells. This pump sends the dark blood to the lungs, where it gets rid of its carbon dioxide and takes on a new oxygen supply. The other pump pushes the "newly conditioned" red blood through the big artery near the heart called the *aorta*—on the first step of its round trip journey.

DOES YOUR HEART LOOK LIKE A VALENTINE HEART?

Valentine hearts come in all sizes. Some are even lacy. Your heart doesn't have lace on it; it is not very large and it is not shaped like a valentine heart.

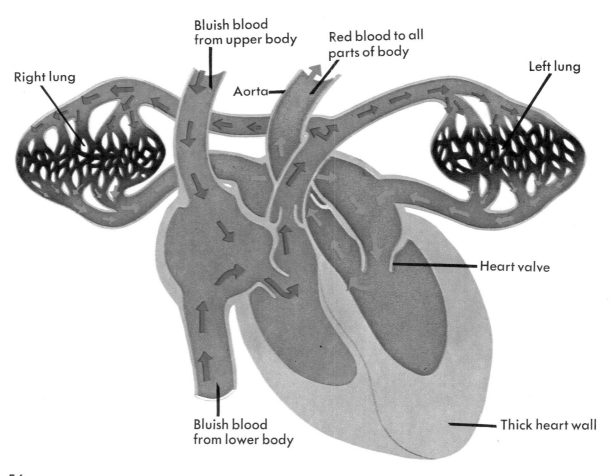

Right lung

Bluish blood from upper body

Aorta

Red blood to all parts of body

Left lung

Heart valve

Bluish blood from lower body

Thick heart wall

Valentine hearts

Make a fist with your hand. That's about the size of your heart. That's about the shape of your heart too.

Most valentine hearts are bigger and prettier than your own heart, but they are not nearly as valuable. You can do without a valentine—but you can't do without your heart!

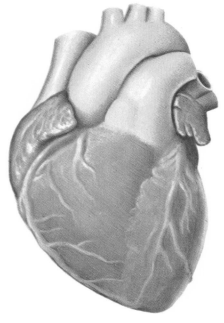

A human heart

DO NICER PEOPLE HAVE BIGGER HEARTS?

Do you have a friend as sweet as sugar? Do you know someone who is as mean as can be? Nice people's hearts are the same size as mean people's. Almost everyone's heart is about the same size and weighs less than one pound.

The only people who have bigger hearts are athletes. That is because constant exercise makes their muscle cells bigger and stronger.

Long ago, people believed that bravery and kindness and love came from the heart. A generous person was said to "have a big heart." But a generous person's heart is no bigger than that of the stingiest man in the world.

HOW DOES BLOOD TRAVEL AROUND YOUR BODY?

Your blood makes a round trip through your body in less than a minute, thousands of times a day. On its way, the blood delivers food and oxygen to your cells. It also picks up wastes from your cells and takes them away.

This is how it makes its fast round trip:

The blood in your body travels through blood vessels.

There are three main kinds of blood vessels—*arteries*, *veins* and *capillaries*. The blood that delivers oxygen and food to your cells travels through blood vessels called arteries.

When the blood flows out of your

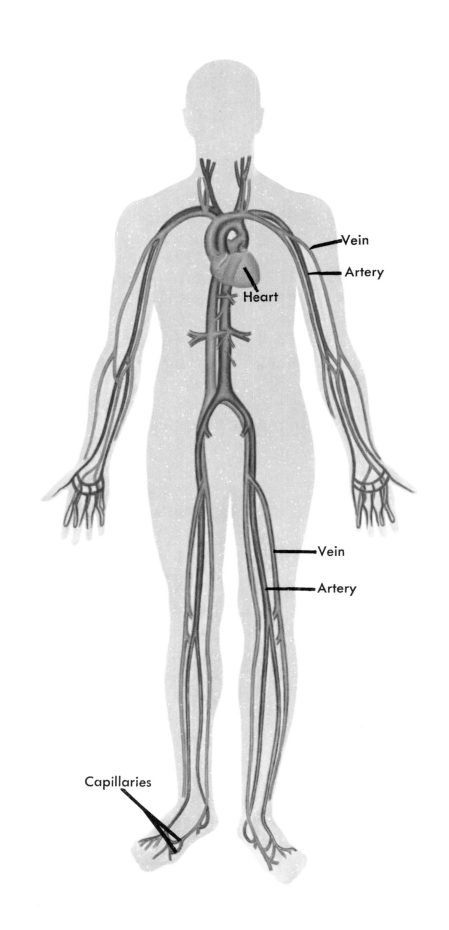

Vein

Artery

Heart

Vein

Artery

Capillaries

heart it goes into the largest arteries. These large arteries branch into smaller ones which branch into still smaller arteries. The blood flows from the smallest arteries into the capillaries.

The capillaries are bridges between the arteries and the veins. They are the tiniest blood vessels, no thicker than a single hair. Their walls are so thin that food (after it has been broken down into molecules) can pass through them. Oxygen can pass through the capillaries too. At the same time, waste products from your cells pass into the capillaries and mix with the blood.

Now the blood, carrying the waste products, travels through another kind of blood vessel. These are the veins. From the tiny capillaries, the blood flows into the smallest veins. The small veins lead to larger and still larger veins, then to the very largest veins that take the blood back to the heart.

WHAT MAKES BLOOD RED?

Oxygen combined with a pigment, called hemoglobin, gives your blood a bright red color. When blood flows

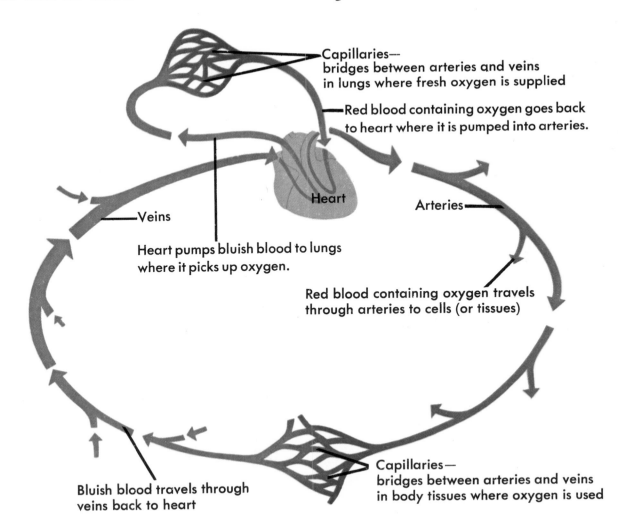

Capillaries—
bridges between arteries and veins in lungs where fresh oxygen is supplied

Red blood containing oxygen goes back to heart where it is pumped into arteries.

Heart

Veins

Arteries

Heart pumps bluish blood to lungs where it picks up oxygen.

Red blood containing oxygen travels through arteries to cells (or tissues)

Bluish blood travels through veins back to heart

Capillaries—
bridges between arteries and veins in body tissues where oxygen is used

through the arteries, it is bright red. When blood flows through veins back to your heart, it is no longer bright red. This blood has delivered oxygen to the cells and has taken on waste materials. Without oxygen, blood takes on a deep dark red color. When the dark red blood in your veins reaches your heart, it is pumped to your lungs.

There, you breathe out the gas called carbon dioxide and breathe in a fresh supply of oxygen. The oxygen turns your blood bright red again.

HOW IS YOUR BLOOD LIKE A SUPERHIGHWAY?

Imagine a highway that leads to every house in town. Everything the houses need to keep them operating smoothly comes along this highway. All the waste materials the houses don't need are removed by this highway.

Blood is your body's highway. Food and oxygen are carried to your cells by blood. Waste materials are taken away from your cells by blood.

Blood travels through your body every second of the day and night.

HOW MUCH BLOOD DO YOU HAVE?

If you weigh about one hundred pounds, you have about seven pounds of blood in your body. All that blood would fill four milk bottles.

If you weigh less, you have less blood. When you become an adult and weigh more, you will have more blood.

WHY DO YOU FEEL THIRSTY?

When your mouth and throat feel dry, you say you are thirsty.

Sometimes you feel thirsty because you have been breathing through your mouth and the air has dried up the saliva. But usually you feel thirsty when the amount of water in your blood gets low.

Your mouth is where you feel the sensation of thirst. You have nerve endings in your throat which send a message to your brain when your throat is dry. The message is, "I'm thirsty."

When you take a drink of water, the water is sent to all the cells of your body through the bloodstream. Eventually, the water goes to the glands that make saliva. In the meantime, you feel less thirsty because the water you drank made your mouth and throat moist.

WHAT ARE BLACK-AND-BLUE MARKS?

You bump your knee, but the blow doesn't break the skin and your knee doesn't bleed. Soon you see the bruise on your knee turn a bluish color.

When you bump your knee, tiny blood vessels inside your skin break. The blood flows out of the blood vessels into the skin. Here the red pigment in the blood is broken down and the color changes from red to yellow, green, and blue. This combination of colors gives the bruise its bluish color.

A "black eye" is caused by broken blood vessels too.

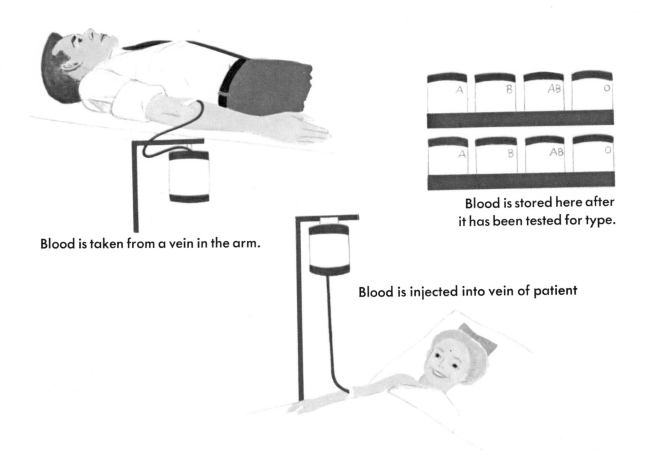

Blood is taken from a vein in the arm.

Blood is stored here after it has been tested for type.

Blood is injected into vein of patient

HOW DOES BLOOD SAVE LIVES?

If someone loses too much blood, it can be very dangerous. Science has found a way to deal with this danger. Blood can be taken from a healthy person and given to someone who has lost too much of it. The blood of the two people must be the same type, or a type that will mix well with the other. Transferring blood in this way is called *blood transfusion.*

Adults sometimes give a pint of their blood to the Red Cross or to hospitals. Their blood is stored away in a blood bank. Then, when a sick or injured person needs some blood to make him well, the right type will be ready for him immediately.

DOES EVERYONE HAVE THE SAME KIND OF BLOOD?

Everyone's blood is made up of blood cells in a liquid called *plasma.* The type of the blood cells may vary, however. You may have one type of blood. Your best friend may have another type. Your blood type will depend on your parents' blood types. Scientists have found that there are four main types of blood.

Although there are different types of blood, many different kinds of people have the same type of blood. A Frenchman may have the same type blood as an Eskimo. A blue-eyed girl may have the same type as a brown-eyed boy. A dark-skinned person may have the same type of blood as a light-skinned person.

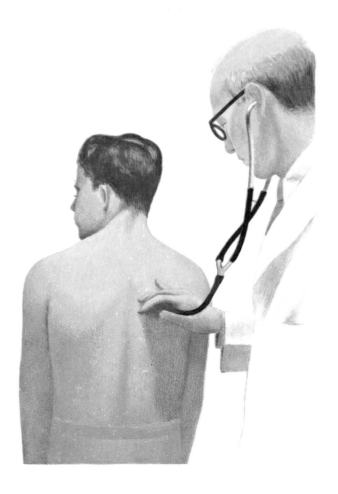

HOW MANY TIMES DOES YOUR HEART BEAT IN A MINUTE?

Right now, as you sit reading this book, your heart is beating about seventy times a minute. When you move about, it beats faster.

Just think how fast a basketball player's heart beats when he's running all over the basketball court. His heart beats about 160 times each minute! It has to work extra hard to bring more blood to his muscles. His muscle cells need more food and oxygen. Your muscle cells do, too, when you exercise.

How many times will your heart beat in your lifetime? If you live to be one hundred years old, your heart will beat more than three-and-one-half billion times!

WHAT DOES YOUR DOCTOR HEAR THROUGH HIS STETHOSCOPE?

Lubb-dup, lubb-dup, lubb-dup. That's the steady rhythm your doctor hears through his stethoscope when he listens to your heart. It's the sound of the strong *valves* of your heart, opening and closing as your heart beats. These heart valves act like one-way doors. They keep the blood flowing in the right direction. When the valves open, blood flows through. When the valves close, blood can't flow backwards. The doctor can tell by the sound of the *lubb-dups* if your heart is working properly.

DOES YOUR HEART EVER REST?

Even when you sleep, your heart must keep blood flowing through your body. Without blood your cells could not live and grow. So it seems as if your heart never has a chance to rest.

Yet your heart is a muscle, and like the muscles of your arms and legs, your heart muscle must rest if it is to do its job properly. And although it cannot get as much rest as your other muscles, your heart does rest ever so briefly between beats.

More About You

WHAT MAKES TEETH HARD?

Your teeth are covered by the hardest material in your body. This hard material is called *enamel*. Although enamel is very strong, it cannot repair itself the way bone can.

HOW DO YOU GET A CAVITY?

Inside the hard enamel covering of your teeth is a soft sensitive center called the *pulp*. There are nerves and blood vessels in the pulp.

After you eat, tiny bits of food are left between your teeth. Usually if these bits of food are not brushed away, the bacteria which thrive on these food particles begin to invade the hard enamel

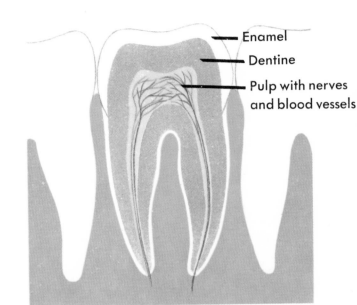

— Enamel
— Dentine
— Pulp with nerves and blood vessels

of your tooth. The hole the bacteria make is a *cavity*. The bacteria not only eat away this hard protective layer, but they also can go right through to the sensitive soft center of your tooth and give you a toothache.

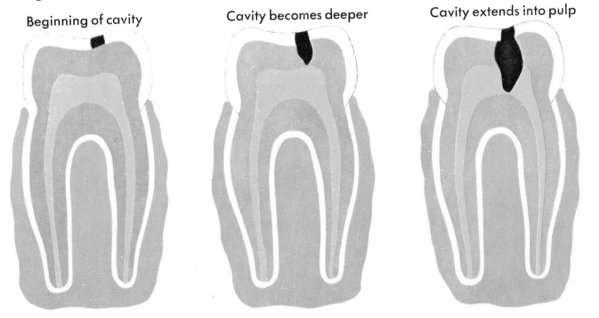

Beginning of cavity   Cavity becomes deeper   Cavity extends into pulp

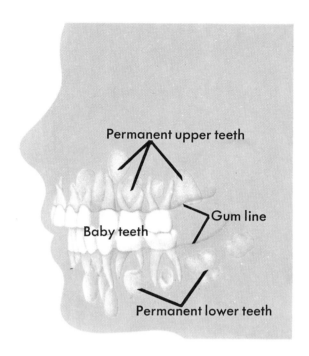

Permanent upper teeth

Baby teeth

Gum line

Permanent lower teeth

WHY DO YOUR TEETH GET LOOSE?

This has probably happened to you already. One day you felt a tooth wobble when you touched it. It was getting loose because a tougher and larger tooth was growing in.

Everyone is born with two sets of teeth. When you were about six months old, your first set of teeth started to come through your gums. These are called baby or "milk" teeth. There are twenty of them. When you are about six, you begin to lose these baby teeth as the permanent teeth begin to push up through the gums, loosening the milk teeth that are in their way.

There are thirty-two teeth in your permanent set. You may not get the last four until you are in your twenties. These are called the *wisdom* teeth, but they have nothing to do with how wise you are.

WHY DO YOU SLEEP?

No one knows exactly why people get sleepy. But everyone knows they do! And everyone knows that sleep is necessary for keeping well and strong. Most people get sleepy around the time they usually go to bed—out of habit.

Every day, many of your cells wear out. When you sleep, your body has a better chance to repair some cells and build new ones.

When you were a baby, you slept about twice as many hours as you stayed awake. Your mother and father stay awake about twice as long as they sleep. You need more sleep than your parents because your body has two big jobs. You not only have to repair or replace worn-out cells but you also have to grow!

What controls your sleeping and your waking? There are two centers in your brain (near the medulla)—a sleep center and a wakefulness center.

WHAT HAPPENS WHEN YOU SLEEP?

Fish and bugs sleep with their eyes open. Not you. You close your eyes when you sleep. Giraffes and horses can sleep standing up. Not you. You usually lie down when you sleep. Bats sleep hanging upside down. You don't. At least, let's hope you don't.

While you sleep, all the parts of your body continue to do their work, though at a slower rate. The heart keeps pumping blood. The lungs keep taking air in and sending air out.

Yet, when you sleep, many strange things happen. Your fingers grow colder and your toes grow warmer. At first you lie fairly quietly, but then you start to move about. Your arms move. So do your legs. Your whole body moves a little. Sometimes you dream.

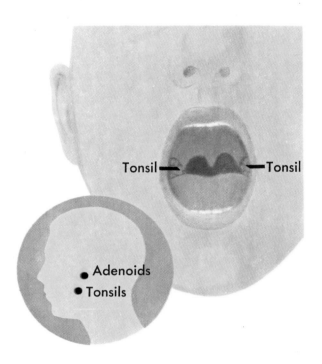

Tonsil— —Tonsil

● Adenoids
● Tonsils

DO YOU NEED YOUR TONSILS?

Your tonsils are located at the back of your mouth—one on each side. They trap harmful bacteria that may enter your nose when you breathe.

Your tonsils are filled with *lymph nodes*, little balls of cells. Lymph nodes act as your body's cleansers. Your body has so many other lymph nodes that your tonsils won't be missed at all if they become infected and have to be taken out.

When tonsils are taken out, *adenoids* are usually removed at the same time. Adenoids are lymph tissues at the back of the nose. When they are infected and swollen, they make your voice sound stuffy and nasal.

DO YOU NEED YOUR APPENDIX?

The *appendix* is a little sac attached to one end of the large intestine. It is about the size of your longest finger.

Scientists think that at one time, thousands of years ago, the appendix served a useful purpose. Now, as far as anyone knows, it is of no use whatsoever to man. In fact if it becomes irritated and inflamed, it must be removed. You can digest your food perfectly well without your appendix.

WHAT IS FEVER?

You wake up one morning and you feel like going right back to sleep. You feel hot and your mouth feels dry. You certainly don't feel like jumping out of bed and hurrying out to play. Your mother pops a thermometer into your mouth for a few minutes. Then she takes it out, looks at it, and says, "You have a *fever*."

You know that when the food in your cells mixes with oxygen to make energy, heat is given off. When you have a fever, your body produces more heat than it gives off. This makes the body temperature rise. A fever is a sign that your body is fighting to try to get rid of whatever is causing an illness.

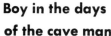

Boy in the days of the cave man

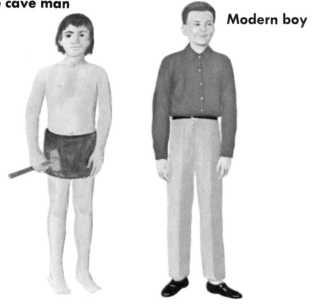

Modern boy

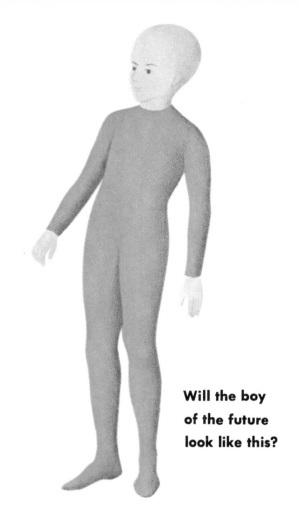

Will the boy of the future look like this?

WHAT WILL PEOPLE LOOK LIKE 100,000 YEARS FROM NOW?

Scientists can't say for certain what the man of the future will look like. Some scientists think man will look something like the figure at the right.

He'll have a smaller face and a bigger nose. He'll have less hair than he does now—in fact, he might even be bald. But there's one good thing about him— he will probably have a bigger brain with many more nerve cells.

Man's face has been gradually getting smaller since cave man days. In that long-ago time, man needed big teeth to tear at big hunks of meat. As his diet changed, his teeth became smaller. So did his jaws, and so did his face!

The man of the future might very well be born without wisdom teeth or tonsils or an appendix, which many doctors say serve no real function now.

ARE YOU EXACTLY LIKE ANYONE ELSE IN THE WHOLE WORLD?

No, there is no one in the world exactly like you. Unless you have an identical twin, there is no one who looks exactly like you. No one talks like you, thinks like you, or likes and hates exactly what you like or hate. No one dreams your dreams except you.

No two people experience the same things or have exactly the same interests.

As special as you are, however, you are like other people in many ways. Sometimes you laugh. Sometimes you cry. Sometimes you feel sad or mad. Everybody does. You need food and warmth and love—exactly like everyone else in the whole world.

Index

(Page numbers in bold type refer to illustrations.)

WHAT IS FEVER?

HOW DO YOU TASTE?

Why do some people have straight hair and others curly hair?

Why are some people left-handed?

WHAT HAPPENS WHEN YOU CRY?

HOW DO YOU REMEMBER WHAT YOU DID YESTERDAY?

Why doesn't food taste as good when you have a cold?

HOW DO YOU GROW?

HOW DO

HOW IS YOUR

Why do people have different colored skins?

Why does your stomach rumble when you're hungry?

WHAT GOES ON INSIDE YOUR BRAIN?

WHAT'S SO FUNNY ABOUT A "FUNNY BONE"?

WHY DO YOU SNEEZE?

What does your doctor hear

What will people look like 100,000 years from now?